OVER 5 YEARS AND THROUGH 51 COUNTRIES, THERE WERE THREE THINGS ROBERT AUBURN DEPENDED ON: HIMSELF, HIS HONDA AND *Castrol*

CASTROL MAKES HIGH PERFORMANCE LUBRICANTS FOR ANY TYPE OF VEHICLE IN EVERY TYPE OF DRIVING CONDITION.

THE LEADING LUBRICANTS SPECIALIST.

Robert B. Auburn

The ENDLESS RIDE

The Pictorial Guide to Worldwide Motorcycle Touring

The ENDLESS RIDE Publications
Newport Beach, CA, USA

The ENDLESS RIDE
The Pictorial Guide to Worldwide Motorcycle Touring

by Robert B. Auburn

Published by: The ENDLESS RIDE Publications, P. O. Box 10044, Newport Beach, CA 92658-0044, USA.

The information and photographs contained in this book are for entertainment only. Anyone who relies upon information herein and sustains a loss, injury, or damage as a proximate result thereof, does so at their own risk. The publisher urges anyone contemplating a trip like that experienced by the author as evidenced herein, to research all aspects of the intended trip in advance.

The ENDLESS RIDE Publications is a completely separate entity from Honda Motor Co., Ltd. and is not affiliated with or a subsidiary of Honda Motor Co. or any other organization.

All photographs are original images taken during actual weather conditions and have not been artificially altered or composited to recreate locations visited or optimum conditions.

This book was created electronically with an Apple Macintosh LC III and an Apple Macintosh Centris 610, except for the Asian language section, which was created manually. Apple is a registered trademark of Apple Corp.

Art Director: M.R. Ogle
Design/Production and Technical Adviser: Patrick Neeman
European Language Coordinators: Herman and Karin ten Cate
Asian Language Coordinator: Sophia Yang
Color Separations by Colourscan, Singapore
Printed by Höfer Communications
Printed in Singapore. $39.95 softcover.

Auburn, Robert B.
The ENDLESS RIDE: The Pictorial Guide to Worldwide Motorcycle Touring /
by Robert B. Auburn — 1st ed.
p. cm.
Preassigned LCCN: 94-094054.
ISBN 0-9639583-4-8
1. Motorcycling 2. Motorcycling–Pictorial works 3. 19-language Parts and Service Phrasebook
4. Motorcycling–Equipment and supplies–Glossaries 5. Travel
I. Title II. Titles: Pictorial Guide to Worldwide Motorcycle Touring

GV1059.5.A83 1994   796.7
                          QBI94-649

About This Book
The Fun and Adventure of Worldwide Motorcycle Touring

As a long-time motorcycle aficionado, I began *The ENDLESS RIDE* in 1989. It was an incredible solo ride, a marathon journey which took more than five years to complete! This world-spanning odyssey would eventually focus in on 51 countries while encompassing 165,000 miles on the *same* **Honda** Magna 700.

If you have never experienced the exhilaration of riding in a foreign country, then the 312 select photographs (uncomposited, unretouched) that appear in this first edition are the next best thing to being there.

If you are an experienced rider, then the new 19-language **Parts and Service Phrasebook** in the *blue pages* will help you to communicate while riding in foreign countries. When I started my ride, there was no phrasebook in existence and I was forced to improvise.

I was in Aschaffenburg, Germany, when my **Honda** needed a valve adjustment. The problem was that I didn't know the German words for intake or exhaust. I did recall, however, that *einfahrt* and *ausfahrt* meant *entrance* and *exit* (I had seen the signs on the autobahn). After repeating these words for a few moments, the young mechanic smiled when he

Buddhist Temple in Pattaya Beach, Thailand.

caught on to what I was trying to say.

It was snowing in Athens, Greece, when I awoke one morning, with a dead battery. After pushing my **Honda** into a garage, I began to wave my arms wildly, jumping up and down, combining theater, diplomacy and philosophy while shouting "jumper cables." My performance must have been on a par with "America's Funniest Home Videos" for everytime I paused for breath, the four Greek mechanics smiled and applauded. Remember, if you cannot get your message across, **raise your voice!**

It's well to remember, that just because you can communicate, your problems may not necessarily be solvable!

For example, I had ridden from dawn at Kathmandu, Nepal, to Sonali on the Indian border and continued on that afternoon to the industrial city of Gorapur. In front of the Hotel Ganges that evening, I inspected my tires for cuts and other signs of potential trouble and it was then that I noticed a machine screw embedded in my rear tire. I broke out my ENGLISH → HINDI translation, but was astonished to discover that no one in that city of 500,000 could fix a tubeless tire. Indians don't use tubeless tires! What this really meant was that there were no cans of pressurized liquid rubber sealer available in India. That evening I used the last can that I had brought with me from Germany. For the remainder of my stay on the Indian sub-continent, I rode with my heart in my mouth.

In March of 1992, I began to collect, in various languages, words & phrases expressing the same service one might need, later to be used in the **Parts and Service Phrasebook**. One year later, Korean was the last of the 19 languages which I compiled with the help of the foremost Honda distributors worldwide.

— *Robert Auburn*

About the Photographer

Robert B. Auburn, a graduate of Stanford University, has had a checkered career: an engineer, an aviator and an expedition cameraman. He has also been an award-winning television producer. His documentary film "Flying the Caribbean," produced with his late wife Marion, was aired as a one-hour ABC Television Prime-Time Special.

Other plaudits include three appearances on the National Geographic's Adventure Series. Over the years, the Auburn films have been exhibited on over 200 television shows.

When not riding in some far corner of the globe, Auburn lives in

Marion and Bob during the filming of "Flying America."

Newport Beach, California, where his hobbies include computer graphics and body surfing.

— *Lynn Newton*

Acknowledgement

I would like to express my appreciation to the following Honda distributors for their gracious reception and cooperation in providing me with the translations used in the new 19-language **Parts and Service Phrasebook.**

AREA	TRANSLATION BY
The Far East	
Japan	Honda of Japan
South Korea	Honda of South Korea
Southeast Asia	
Thailand	Honda of Thailand
Singapore	Honda of Singapore
Australia	Honda of Australia*
India	Honda of India
Africa	Honda of Morocco
Europe	
England	Honda of the United Kingdom
Portugal	Honda of Portugal
Spain	Honda of Spain
Greece	Honda of Greece
Italy	Honda of Italy
France	Honda of France
Germany	Honda of Germany
The Netherlands	Honda of The Netherlands
Scandinavia	
Denmark	Honda of Denmark
Sweden	Honda of Sweden
Norway	Honda of Norway
Finland	Honda of Finland
North America	
Mexico	Honda of Mexico

*As the meaning of English words often changes from continent to continent, I asked Honda of Australia to verify the English words and phrases as they pertained to Australia.

I'm greatly indebted to Victor Kotowitz, an editorial artist with The Los Angeles Times, for creating the computer-generated maps used in this pictorial guide.

Neil Kenney and Dennis Smith of Castrol, London, U. K., and Bryan Baldwin of Castrol, Bangkok, Thailand, were particularly helpful in supplying me with technical data which greatly facilitated the publication of this book.

A special thanks to English Heritage for permitting me to take photographs of my **Honda** inside Bolsover Castle. To obtain a free brochure on English Heritage events, write: Special Events Section, Keysign House, 429 Oxford Street, London W1R, England.

Finally, I cannot adequately express my dependence on and appreciation for the countless foreign government facilities I encountered: the ministries of information, the tourist development boards, the tourist authorities and the departments of antiquity. They were all kind enough to supply me with written documents enabling me to obtain photographs which under normal conditions would have been off-limits.

At a camel market in the Nubian Desert, Egypt.

Table of Contents

Once you have seen with your eyes

you may judge with your heart

– an ancient Thai proverb

FROM
KASBAHS
TO
KANGAROOS

Morocco to Australia

The hub of the ancient city of Meknes, Morocco, is built around the massive Bab El Mansour, the marvelous entrance-way to Moulay Ismail's 17th century capital. Beautifully carved, this arabesque arch is the most impressive entryway in all of North Africa.

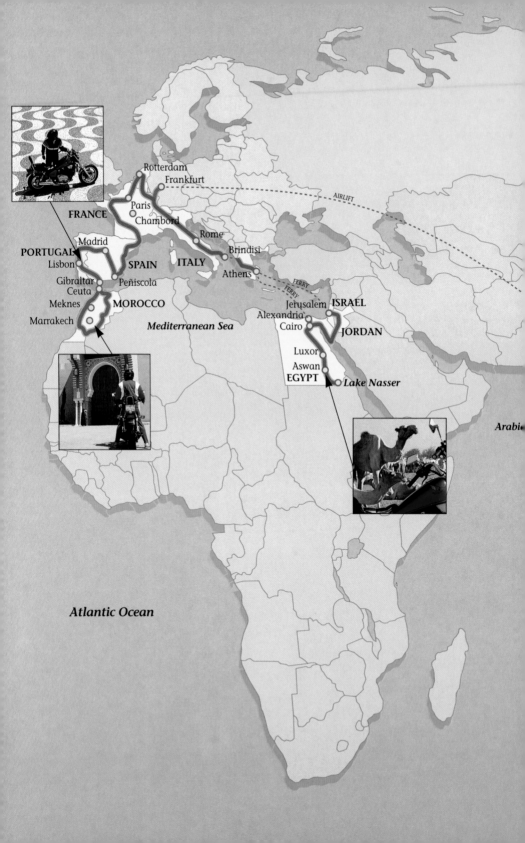

(Far right inset) **My "second camera-man,"** a Nikon 801 with a radio-controlled shutter release, had an effective range of 100 yards. I used it for photographing my **Honda** as well as for capturing wild animals in Thailand, Alaska, Australia, Egypt and India.

(Right) **The Dancing Bears of Agra, India.**

(Below) **Don't eat the transmitter!** One afternoon I rode out to the small elephant corral at Pattaya Beach, Thailand, to see the new arrivals. To my left was *"Princess,"* a baby female elephant whose mother had been killed by tigers. She had a bottomless pit for a stomach and ate all the bananas I could provide. The adult male to my right appeared far more interested in my transmitter than in the bananas I was offering!

(Far right) **The wild side of "Down Under."** Wombats, wallabies, kangaroos and most of the wildlife of Australia are nocturnal creatures that come to life once the sun begins to set. *"Big Fella,"* a gray 'roo, was, however, a daytime panhandler and always eager to scrounge a meal. As he was ravenous and his actions somewhat unpredictable, I kept my tinted visor down during feeding to prevent him from accidentally putting his paw into my eye. Note the transmitter in my right hand.

The Wall at Dawn

I had ridden my Honda around the celebrated walled
cities of Carcassonne in France, Avila in Spain and Obidos
in Portugal, but there was something about the ochre
mud walls of Marrakech, Morocco, that impressed me as
none of the others had. Was it those irregular holes that
appeared every now and then, placed at odd elevations,
holes that, I learned later, were designed to be fitted with
tree branches from which scaffolding could be hung? Or
did its appeal lay in the fact that it was remote, primitive,
unique?

(Above) **The Place of the Dead** (the name was derived from the barbaric custom of impaling the head of an executed criminal on a nearby wall). The storied Jamma El Fna Square in Marrakech, Morocco, hosts a fascinating market every afternoon, selling everything from bubble gum to guaranteed love potions. But night doesn't fall on Marrakech, it *rises*. From the secure balconies overlooking the square, you can watch as dancers, acrobats, snake charmers, and tame monkeys entertain the crowd to the throbbing beat of drums and the wailing of flutes. The fact that this same show goes on night after night, virtually unchanged over the centuries is unique.

(Right) **Intricate, hand-set mosaic tiles** display breathtaking artistry in a street fountain in Meknes, Morocco. Moslem women prefer public fountains to piped-in water. The community fountains serve as a gathering place for gossip seekers.

10

The opulent Royal Palace gates of Berber Marrakech. The function of the full gate is for horse-drawn carriages of state, though openings now-a-days are rare. The smaller doorway cut into the gate on the right is for pedestrian traffic.

Blue is the color of Fez, Morocco. In cramped Fez el Bali, old Fez, houses press so tightly upon each other that only foot traffic can file their way through the maze of narrow alleyways.

(Above) **Within the ancient walls of** the city of Fez is a sight which you should not miss — the honeycombs of vegetable stain in which renowned Moroccan leather is dipped. Standing calf deep in dye, tanners soak cowhides, goatskins, and camelskins for eventual use as slippers, belts, wallets, and saddles. As I climbed the age-old stairs to an observation point, my guide gave me some fresh mint to place under my nose. "Take it," he said. "One of the ingredients used is bird droppings." This vile smell explains why the tanning vats are always located next to the aged wall and on the *downwind* side of the city.

(Left) **The official language** of Morocco is Arabic although French is the language of business but sometimes the language of gesture is as clear as the spoken word. Placing my hands together in the form of a small triangle, I asked a water vender, compete with brass cups and goatskin bag, for directions to the campground located within the Palace walls.

13

Mud-brick Skyscrapers of the Sahara

On the southern slopes of the High Atlas Mountains of Morocco and bordering the Sahara on the north is the deserted kasbah of Ait Ben Haddou, the gem of the High Atlas. Built hundreds of years ago when camel caravans criss-crossed the arid Sahara, the kasbah, or fortress, served as a motel for weary travelers. With the coming of paved roads, this out-of-the-way kasbah fell into disuse and was eventually abandoned

(Inset) **A young Tuwareg-dressed warrior** brandishes a vintage rifle.

(Top) **On the route of the fabled silk caravans.** Built in 1757, the mud-brick kasbah, in the town of Ouarzazate in the northern Sahara, bakes in the noontime sun. This red-earth citadel was once fortified as were most of the Saharan villages. During fierce tribal wars, sentries kept watch from the mud-brick watchtowers. Today, once the cool breath of evening sweeps away the last vestige of oppressive daytime heat, these flat rooftops serve as entertainment terraces.

(Right) **Although I had three locks** and an alarm system on my **Honda**, Hassan, with his wicked, curved dagger, was my most dependable deterrent in Marrakech. While on duty, he never slept. As a result, I never lost anything. The fact that he was 6′ 4″ and weighed 240 pounds didn't hurt either.

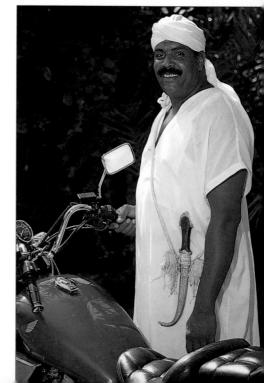

16

Proud and independent,
hooded Berber horsemen await
the start of a "Fantasia."

Windmills of Don Quixote

I spent a night camping beneath an aging wind-mill at Consuegra, Spain. Tired after an all day ride, I was rocked to sleep by the steady creaking and groaning of the lattice work arms, moving as if tugged by unseen forces.

The Windmills of Campo de Cristana. South of Toledo, I rode into the *Castillo* and *La Mancha* country of Spain, a desolate and parched corner of Iberia left over from another era. Revolving a mill into the wind during the time of Don Quixote was always an exciting event to watch.

After climbing the narrow, circular stairway to the roof, the miller would open a small window to determine the direction of the wind. Then the overhead, wooden beams, which served as bearings, would be coated with fat. Finally, a team of oxen would be harnessed to the "pig tail" protruding from the rear of the roof and with shouts of encouragement from the teamsters, the oxen would slowly turn the sail-wrapped arms into the wind. This method of roof rotation was unique to the windmills of Spain.

21

(Above) **A commanding location.** Built on a narrow isthmus, the Mediterranean castle at Peñiscola is like no other in Spain. The old fortress will be remembered, however, more for events than for its location because of schismatic Papa Luna (Pope Luna). When Pope Luna was appointed to that honorable position, the Vatican already had two other popes. Since none of the three wanted to abdicate, the problem was eventually solved by naming a fourth and absolute Pope. Pope Luna died in his castle believing to the end that *he* was the legitimate Pope.

(Right) **Wrought-iron street lamps** and flower-filled balconies line the narrow, one-way streets in the Old City of Peñiscola, Spain. The small pebbled riding surface of the lanes was fine in dry weather; after a downpour this surface had a tendency to become as slippery as ice.

(left) **Grim towers of a walled city.** A pleasant four-hour ride northward from Madrid, Spain, is the medieval fortress of Avila, a city entirely encompassed within ancient watchtowers, knightly gates, and timeless bulwarks. Of the once 10,000 "Castles in Spain," today, barely 2,500 survive.

(above and right) **High on a barren, wind-swept hill,** gazing down on a sleepy Spanish village, is the castle of Belmonte. Restored to its original state, this castle served as a colorful backdrop for the motion picture film "El Cid."

Mosaic Waves Splash the Waterfront
Cascais, Portugal

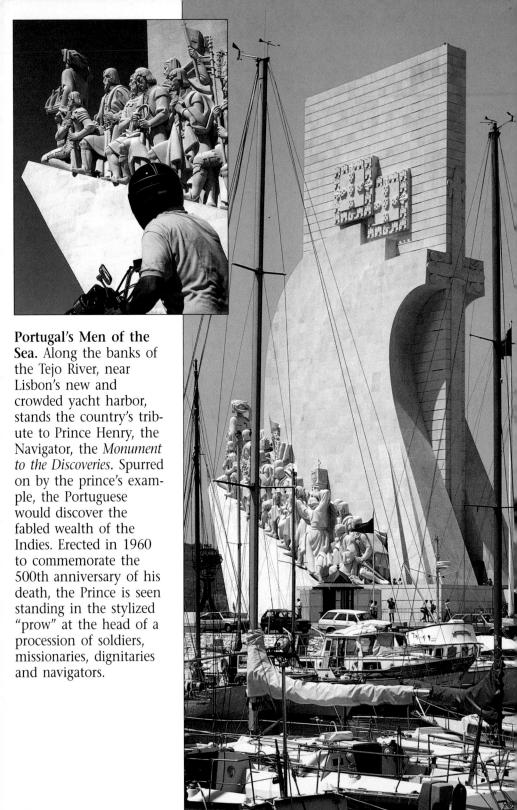

Portugal's Men of the Sea. Along the banks of the Tejo River, near Lisbon's new and crowded yacht harbor, stands the country's tribute to Prince Henry, the Navigator, the *Monument to the Discoveries*. Spurred on by the prince's example, the Portuguese would discover the fabled wealth of the Indies. Erected in 1960 to commemorate the 500th anniversary of his death, the Prince is seen standing in the stylized "prow" at the head of a procession of soldiers, missionaries, dignitaries and navigators.

sbon's princely ortress. Dawn and irror-perfect re- ections surround the ately Tower of lem. Built early in e 16th century, the wer is notable for e fact that the mplicity and robust- ss of a fortress fit rfectly with the arm and beauty of a ork of art. It was om this location that rtugal's most famous plorers embarked on eir historic voyages to the unknown.

Chambord – The Majestic Hunting Lodge

The largest chateau in the Loire Valley of France was the residence of King Francois I (with 440 rooms and 365 fireplaces). Its structure is said to be of Italian inspiration, the work of the renowned architect Leonardo da Vinci who had been employed by the King. When visiting Chambord, you can't escape the feeling that this chateau is pure *macho*, a sportsman's lodge, on whose grounds wild boar still roam.

(Right) **Generations of pilgrims** have sought curios along the Grande Rue, their footsteps having worn smooth the flagstones with which Mont-St-Michel's "Main Street" is paved.

(Below) **The best vantage point** to witness a rarity of nature, the famous tides of Mont-St-Michel, France, is from the lock over the meandering Couesnon River. At low tide, the treacherous quicksands — which have claimed many a victim — are exposed. During hightide, most of what is seen now will be submerged, except for that medieval island of faith, crowned by the Abbey of Mont-St-Michel.

ike a **phantom castle** in the
ky, Mont-St-Michel stands on a
nall island about a mile off the
rench coast. It has been in oper-
ion since the 10th century. A
useway connecting it to
ormandy was opened in 1936,
cilitating the one million visi-
ors who flock yearly to this spot.
he once famous "wall of water"
o longer occurs, however, peak
ood tides have been measured
aveling a respectable 24 miles in
 hours.

(Above and right) **Holland's past and future** intermix at Rotterdam's sea-faring harbor. Colorful pubs and terraces line the open-air Inland Navigation Museum while futuristic, cube houses peer down on historic sailing ships.

(Far right) **To find the functioning windmills** of Holland, I had to ride about thirty minutes southeast of Rotterdam to the town of Kinderjijk. Here the windmills unceasingly grind grain, saw timber, and pump water just as they have for the last 200 years.

Gladiator-haunted Stadium of Rome

Its real name was the Flavian Amphitheater, but the name Coliseum was unquestionably chosen from a colossus of Nero in the vicinity. The 1,900-year-old amphitheater has seen contests with wild animals and gladiatorial duels. Even fake naval battles took place on its flooded floor. Although stone scavengers, pollution, looters, and earthquakes have extracted their toll, the Coliseum still remains "the sight" to see in Rome.

(Below) **The ageless Coliseum** still serves Rome, but this time as a traffic circle for the city's one million cars.

The Fountain of the Four Rivers located in the Plazza Navona, Rome, was an idea of Bernini. Of the four great rivers depicted, my ride would eventually take me to the Danube in Austria, the Nile in Egypt, and the Ganges in India. Only the Rio de la Plata eluded me.

The Trevi Fountain first bubbled forth in Rome during the 18th century and at that time the waters associated with it were said to have a spa-like quality. "Rather a waterfall than a fountain," Shelley once wrote. And an old saying still persists: "turn your back to the fountain, throw a coin over your shoulder and you'll return." Well, maybe.

Everyone Loved It!

In the Swiss capital of Bern, my **Honda** Magna 700 appealed to the young, to the old, and even to their pets.

Anniversary flags ripple in the breeze. August 1, 1991, was the 800th anniversary of the founding of Bern, the capital of Switzerland, and the arcades lining the medieval Old Town were an explosion of color. Riding down the cobblestoned Kramgasse, I was enroute to the clock tower to watch its famous animated figures "come to life." Of all the photographs in this book, this one was to be the most time-consuming as I had to wait out nearly two weeks of thunderstorms to finally get a bright sunny day.

Valley of the Waterfalls. Situated in a rugged glacial valley, along the banks of the foaming Lutschine River, the chalet village of Lauterbrunner, Switzerland, is the site of 72 waterfalls, including the famous Staubbach and the underground Trummelbach.

A cool morning ride. Southward from of the alpine resort village of Lauterbrunner, Switzerland, the narrow glacial valley road skirts some of the most magnificent and loftiest peaks in Europe. Note the parasailer in the upper right hand corner.

Remnant from another age. Tortured blue-ice pinnacles, 60 to 100 feet high, line the face of the Upper Grindelwald Glacier, a Swiss river of ice that is melting faster than it is advancing.

Legacy of a Dazzling Past

Ravaged by Time and War, the lovely Parthenon still stands atop an ancient hill dominating the skyline of Athens, Greece. Gunpowder, religious strife, smog, acid rain, and disrespect have devestated this once mighty temple of Athena, down-grading it to the still lovely, but broken fragment of its former self. From Philopappou Hill, where once Socrates was held prisoner, I watched as new scaffolding, steel cranes, and legions of workmen toiled methodically in a modern day rescue attempt to restore the once mighty Parthenon — an original "masterpiece" of classical Greek architecture.

(Right) **Parading from Parliament** in the center of downtown Athens to the Tomb of Greece's Unknown Soldier at Sintagma Square, the showy *Evzoni* guards strut a stately pace.

(Below right) It's an all day ride from Athens, Greece, to the vast monastic community at Meteora, the second most visited site on the Greek mainland. Lofty solitude was the ultimate reward for the 14th century Byzantine monks who, toiling unceasingly, built twenty-four virtually inaccessible monasteries. Only five remain today.

(Far right) **Peter, the panhandling pelican.** The chief attraction on the Adriatic Island of Mykonos was Peter, the feathered fisherman, whose lifestyle was second to none. Every morning, he toured the fish markets, flapping his wings and making all kinds of noise until someone finally noticed and rewarded him with a freshly caught fish. Then, he would slowly waddle uphill to the cafes where he would hustle drinks. Islanders said his favorite drink was soda water. Perhaps. But I once saw him down a glass of beer in a single swallow!

48

An enigma wrapped in mystery, the royal funeral barge of Pharaoh Khufu (Cheops) was an astonishing discovery in 1954. Constructed 4,600 years ago from Lebanese cedar, the solar boat, the oldest vessel in existence, is 143 feet in length and is sewn together transversely. Exhumed from a pit near the base of the Great Pyramid of Giza (Cairo), it's housed today in an air-conditioned museum. The 1,224 pieces of this vessel were painstakingly reassembled prior to the advent of computers. Noted for its high, elegantly tapered stem-and-stern posts, this royal barge evolved from Egypt's most ancient craft: the papyrus river raft of the Nile.

The top line translates as "Alexandria Customs." Egypt was the only country, in which I rode, that required that I place a temporary Egyptian license over my California license plate. To obtain this temporary license, I had to "deposit" $40. When the time finally came for me to leave Egypt, I applied for a refund only to discover that the word "refund" does not exist in the Egyptian language.

The Golden Era. Egyptian Pharaohs, wearing hand-crafted golden helmets, gazed down at me from a wall of hieroglyphics at the Temple of Karnak, Luxor, Egypt. But that was then, this is now. Protected by a space-age Arai F-1 helmet and astride my **Honda** Magna 700, I rode into the former capital of the Middle Kingdom, located 400 miles south of Cairo and on the east bank of the Nile River.

Sentinels of Silence

As dawn's first fingers touched the Temple of Luxor, I strolled toward two immense colossi carved from pink granite representing the Pharaoh Ramesses II seated on his throne. The Colossi are 51 feet in height and were once flanked by a pair of obelisks. Today, only the left one remains. *(Above)* The right obelisk was taken to Paris, in 1836, by King Philippe and now stands at the Place de la Concorde.

(Top left) **Bargaining, a way of life** in Egypt. Just outside of Luxor one afternoon, I ran out of fuel and had to be rescued by a donkey-drawn refueling cart. After some haggling, we finally settled on 90 piasters per liter (about $1.08 a gallon). When you buy fuel in this manner, remember, never ask about "the final filter" as you won't like the answer!

(Bottom left) **In the Valley of the Kings,** Luxor, Egypt. The eminent Ramesseum, constructed by Pharaoh Ramesses II, was built with such perfection and on such an lavish scale that, in its heyday, it surpassed all other temples. In the 19th century, the English poet Shelley made fun of the dead King's mighty boasts with his poem *Ozymandias.*

"....
My name is Ozymandias,
  King of Kings
Look on my works, ye
  Mighty and despair!
Nothing beside remains.
  Round the decay
Of that colossal wreck,
  boundless and bare
The lone and level sands
  stretch far away."

(Far left) **A forest of columns whose** dimensions and plays of light and shadow still produce incredible emotions, the Hypostyle Hall at Luxor has withstood the ravages of time.

Colossi of Memnon. On the west bank of the Nile River at Luxor are seated the Colossi of Memnon, all that remains today of the burial temple of Amenophis III. These time-worn statues, which once marked the entrance, are 63 feet in height. The southern Colossus is in far better condition than the northern one, which at dawn once used to emit a wailing sound when struck by the early morning wind.

Overnight at the "Camel Motel"

Completely worn out after an arduous 45-day trek (from the Sudan to the south or a two week trail drive from the Red Sea to the east), these nomadic "ships-of-the-desert" will spend a night at the "Camel Motel" in Daraw, Egypt, before going on the auction block the next day. The overnight rate, which includes a policeman, is $1 per camel per night. The white and pink colored animals are the perennial favorites and will fetch about 2,000 Egyptian pounds ($600) while younger camels, used primarily for food, will bring about 500 Egyptian pounds ($150).

A Desolate Moonscape

f all the deserts I rode (the Sahara of North Africa, the Sinai of Egypt, the Negev f Israel, the Thar of Western India, the Western Desert of Australia, the Sonora of lexico, and the Mojave of California), none was more godforsaken than the ubian Desert of Egypt. Not a village, not a house, not a tent, not a tree, not even withered blade of grass broke the monotonous landscape. With no fueling stops enroute, I had to carry extra fuel on the 170-mile ride from Aswan, gypt, to the Temple of Abu Simbel on the border with the Sudan.

The mighty monuments of Ramesses II have endured for 3,300 years beside the Nile at Abu Simbel. Dwarfed by the 67-foot magnificent Colossi, visitors marvel at the reconstructed temple which preserves the pharaoh as ever young and vigourous. Falcons, a mark for both the king and Ra (the sun god), stand guard at the base while carved baboons raise their paws to salute the rising sun. Once threatened to be drowned by the rising waters of the Nile, Abu Simbel, is perched today 200 feet higher and 690 feet further inland than its original site as the result of a massive multi-nation rescue which took 4 ½ years and 40 million dollars to accomplish.

rode back to Aswan just as the setting sun was turning the Nile into a ver of gold. During the day, I had ridden 340 miles across one of the ost inhospitable landscapes imaginable to see a wonder from an ancient orld. Now, with a cold Stella Beer in my hand, I relaxed and watched eless *feluccas*, devoid of tourists, return to their moorings.

An Arid World Untouched by Man

The isolated **Sinai Peninsula** of **Egypt** is a region of polychrome colors and unbelievable stillness, of searing heat and freezing nights. It's the Biblical land of the "burning bush" and of trackless deserts, a region so alien that the Bible recalls that Moses and the Israelites wandered the Sinai for forty years and never once reported seeing an authorized **Honda** dealer!

A City Half as Old as Time

I know of no city, either ancient or modern, that offers such a breathtaking first glimpse as Petra, Jordan's rose-colored city in the desert. Petra is graced by 2,000 year-old rock-hewn ruins and I planned to ride my **Honda** down the narrow, mile-long "Siq" (siq means pass) to the sites below. But at the last moment my permission was canceled on the grounds that "my motorcycle would pollute the atmosphere" (my **Honda** Magna 700 was sold in California with an emissions-control device attached — politics!).

Carrying my helmet, the next morning I hiked down the boulder-strewn cleft to the ageless "Treasury" far below. This impressive sandstone structure stands 130 feet tall and was carved in the face of a rugged cliff by workmen suspended from ropes who literally worked their way "from top to bottom." Legend has it that pirates once hid their plunder in the urn near the upper level of the temple. Apparently, the nomadic Bedouin tribes who live in the deserted temples nearby believed this ageless fable as the urn was pockmarked with rifle fire in unsuccessful attempts to break it open.

Where Lawrence of Arabia Once Rode

Near Wadi Rum, Jordan, I stopped by a Bedouin tent, and (with traditional hospitality) was invited for tea. Watching my young host fan the coals, I noticed that he was wearing a gold Rolex watch. Bedouins at one time used to measure their wealth in camels, goats, wives, and the number of children they sired, though not necessarily in that order. Now it's the materialism of fast pickup trucks, television sets, and very expensive gold watches. Their lifestyle is changing rapidly as the 21st century approaches.

(Far left) **The Camel Corps of the** Desert Police was originally set up to maintain peace between the warring Bedouin tribes. However, in today's world, its priorities have changed. Wearing the traditional costume of a desert tracker, Salem told me that his main job now consisted of tracking down drug smugglers bound for the rich markets along the shores of the Mediterranean.

(Left and above) **The Golden Heart** of the Old City of Jerusalem, Israel, contains the Dome of the Rock Mosque. This view is seen from the Church of the Ascension half way up the slopes of the Mount of Olives.

Going One-on-One with Buddha

(Right) **Unable to bless my Honda** Magna 700, a Sadhu or Holy one at noisy Durbar Square, Kathmandu, Nepal, suggested that I go to nearby Bodhnath Monastery and spin a Tibetan prayer wheel.

(Below right) **Prayer flags fluttering in** the breeze at the Buddhist "Monkey Temple," just to the West of Kathmandu, carry the same blessings as do the prayer wheels. The question-mark-like nose of Buddha is actually the Nepalese number 1 and represents oneness. Fixed between Buddha's piercing eyes is a smaller third eye symbolizing Buddha's clairvoyant power.

(Page 72) **The enormous prayer wheels** at the sacred "Monkey Temple" in Kathmandu are usually revolved very slowly, but as I wanted Buddha's undivided attention, I grabbed each prayer wheel with both hands and literally sent them into orbit! As I began my requests ("Buddha protect me from those Indian bicyclists, those bicycle rickshaws..."), the Tibetan villagers who had gathered to watch roared with laughter!

he Buddhist Monastery at Bodhnath was an easy half-hour ride east
om Katmandu. When I arrived, the place was swarming with tourists,
any circling the stupa's whitewashed base in the customary clockwise
ection. Each visitor held out a right hand to spin a minature, recessed
ayer wheel which carries a sacred prayer or mantra, "live long and pros-
r." However, for my particular purpose, the mob at Bodhnath was too big

"Your helmet, Sir." At the posh Meridie Hotel in New Delhi, India, I lived like Maharaja on a mere biker's budge

(Left) **The City Palace at Udaipur** in Rajasthan, India, is really four separate Palaces, bound together by harmony of design.

(Below) **If you are going to live it up** somewhere in India, do it at the posh Lake Palace Hotel, Udaipur. Situated on a small island in magnificent Lake Pichola, rooms start at $100 and rise quickly to $500 for what the management calls an "historic suite," (whatever that means). If you cannot afford to spend a night, then try lunch — the service will take you back to the days of the British Raj!

No State in India is more popular with visiting riders than Rajasthan on the northwest frontier. Though the narrow road surfaces are rough and the major highways are often just one lane, the rewards of motorcycling in this state far outweigh any minor inconvenience.

(Right) **When Prince Albert visited Jaipur** in 1853, all the structures and walls within the Old City were painted pink, an earthy color that signifies welcome. With the arrival of air pollution, the pink has gradually been oxidized to its present day ochre.

(Far right) **The Hawa Mahal,** or Wind Palace, Jaipur. Five stories high, the lovely Hawa Mahal contains hundreds of octagonal windows and small stone screens. And it's all of one room deep! Behind this facade, the ladies of the royal court sat to catch the late afternoon breeze *(hawa).*

Studded with spikes, the city gates of Udaipur were designed to discourage opposing army elephants from pushing against them.

Marvel in Marble
The Taj Mahal, Agra, India

The Taj Mahal, begun in 1630, hardly needs an introduction to visiting riders in India since it is the raison-de-etre for coming to Agra. Created by Shah Jahan as a memorial to his Queen, Mumtaz Mahal, the monument, constructed of white marble, took 22 years to complete.

(Right)
Varanasi, the holiest city in India. With the copper glow of dawn lighting the Ganges, Hindu pilgrims flock to the "ghats" to wash and bathe in India's "River of Faith."

Unexpected Departure!

(Above) **The large headlines in** *The Times Of India* told the tragic tale. The sequence of events leading up to the destruction of the mosque at Ayodhya by religious zealots was to set off the worst communal rioting in India since its partitioning in 1947. Hundreds were killed and thousands injured in weeks of rioting.

(Left) **I was trapped in the city of** Poona, 72 miles to the east of Bombay. My only escape lay by rail to Madras, 750 miles away. At the railway station, my **Honda** was "wrapped" while I stood in endless lines to get a ticket. At every unscheduled stop during the long night, anxious eyes peered into the darkness. When we finally rolled into Madras 28 hours later, I went out in search of a cold beer!

(Far left) **Wearing the colorful Adat Bali**, or national costume, a young Balinese rider pauses in front of Ubud's accommodation board located at the top end of Monkey Forest Road. With spartan, clean rooms going for $4 a night and new **Hondas** available for $4 a day, Bali is very much a rider's delight.

(Left) **A creature from the sea** decorates a fishing outrigger arriving at turquoise Padang Bay, Bali's Mecca for scuba divers.

(Below) **On the black volcanic sand beach** at tropical Kusamba, coolie-clad fishermen, toting time-worn bags filled with sea water, watch as the dawn fishing fleet returns.

(Above) **Although Indonesia was a signatory** to the carnet that I carried, Customs would not permit me to temporarily import my Magna 700 into Indonesia. So while my **Honda** was being shipped to Australia, I jetted to Bali and rented a new Astra Prima, a **Honda** Dream II look-alike with a name change.

(Right) **Through a split, stone gate. Honda** riding on Bali is both sun-filled and inexpensive. The price of fuel during my visit was a scant 90 cents a gallon, a far cry from the outrageous $5.30 a gallon I paid in Italy!

(Above) **An island of stone temples.** Perched precariously on a rocky outcropping off Bali's southern tip, Tanah Lot, the Sea Shrine, faces a relentless sea.

(Left) **Rising out of the ashes.** Balinese cremations are festive holiday occasions as the soul of the departed is set free from its earthly constraints during the ceremony. Cremations involving royalty or high-caste families are always well publicized beforehand but to catch a smaller, more intimate Balinese ceremony, just be on your **Honda** at the right place and right time.

Lonely Land of Far Horizons

Australia's outback tracks are best viewed with caution. Dangerous during the "dry" when daytime temperatures soar to 140 °F, 60 °C, they are just as formidable in the "wet" when the rain turns the red, dusty track into an all but impassable sea of muck. As I studied my map, a "ute" (an Australian pickup truck) roared up. "You're not going to take that track are you?" shouted the driver. "I hadn't planned to." "Good," he replied, and without any further explanation, put his "ute" in gear and roared off in a cloud of bull dust. To this day I've always wondered, what did he know that I didn't?

South of Darwin at the Top End of Australia, I came upon a forest of tall cathedral-like termite mounds. Constructed by insects known as white ants, these abandoned structures have withstood the monsoon rains of the "wet" and the brush fires of the "dry." Note the charred trees from previous "dry" brush fires.

Life in the back of beyond. A bigger-than-life wall mural, depicting the early days in Australia, decorates a modern supermarket in Alice Springs in the Northern Territory.

Wheeled Drovers of Australia

A 133-foot-long road train dwarfs two Aussie riders near the Barkly Roadhouse in the Northern Territory. Used primarily for hauling cattle, these double-decked road trains, capable of transporting 200 head, have replaced the century-old trail-drives in the Outback of Australia.

Caution! A Koala's claws are as sharp as razors. The word "Koala" is aboriginal in origin and means "no drink" thus describing Australia's lovable marsupials that draw water from food, the leaves of certain types of eucalyptus or gum trees. Found primarily in Queensland, New South Wales, and Victoria, Koalas are, in essence, defenseless when on the ground.

An ever present roadside danger, the Australian kangaroo leaps before it looks. Native to only the "Land Down Under," the fifty odd species of kangaroo range in size from the one-pound, fully-grown musky rat kangaroo to the 7-foot tall red variety. Most large kangaroos have multiplied over the years — much to the delight of tourists and to the dismay of ranchers who consider them as nothing more than an annoyance.

He Walked
on the Ocean Floor
for 40 Years

(Left) **At the seaport of Broome** on the Pearling Coast of Western Australia, I met Henry, an aboriginal diver and one of the few survivors of that turbulent era. One afternoon over beers, he told me his story. "When our Japanese diver died from the sickness (bends), I asked the Captain if I could become the next diver. He and a mate threw me overboard. Luckily, I was a good swimmer and I swam back to the ship. After pulling me onboard, the Captain told me that I had just passed 'the test' for becoming the next diver."

(Below) **Typhoon-ravaged grave markers** of the Japanese pearl divers stood in stark contrast to the shiny, new, black headstones in Broome, Western Australia. Prior to World War II, Japanese divers monopolized the Australian oyster beds. The much sought-after prize in those days was the mother-of-pearl shell used in the button making industry. Opening an oyster shell and finding a pearl in that era was just an uneventful discovery.

Australia's Great Technicolor Stones

(Right) **Polished by the wind and the rain** over the millennia, Ayers Rock (rising 1,143 feet out of the scorched red desert of the Outback) is Australia's greatest tourist attraction.

(Below) **Just after sunrise and** again just before sunset, Ayers Rock puts on a dazzling display. The reason for the color change is both simple and bizarre: the rock which is primarily hematite, an iron ore, is rusting. As the sun's rays strike the iron oxide particles at a low angle, the rock flares a brilliant red.

Multi-banded Wave Rock is one of Western Australia's unique sights. Rising nearly [ ] feet, the wave's flowing stripes are caused by "run-off" waters, charged with carbon-[ ]es and iron hydroxide. As [ ]ave Rock was not enclosed [ ]y a fence, I took a [ ]oment before leaving [ ] "Ride the Wave."

Early one morning, I rode to the Sydney Opera House to see if I could photograph my **Honda** Magna near their north steps. "It'll cost you $500." The PR man, after looking at my portfolio of photographs, apparently surmised that I was working for Honda. As $500 meant gasoline for one month, I declined his offer and rode to the north side of the harbor. Jumping the curb, I rolled out onto Finger Wharf which has a commanding view of the waterfront. When a couple of passing policemen looked my way but said nothing, I relaxed and broke out my fishing rod. Later, as the afternoon clouds started to gather, I got the photograph I wanted and saved $500!

The Second Annual Australian Grand Prix

(*Above*) **At torturous Honda corner** on Phillip Island, off the Southern Coast of Australia, I focused on Wayne Gardner (10) just as he started to accelerate. Running a close second was teammate Mick Doohan (9). During the Grand Prix, straight-away speeds often exceeded 180 mph while on tight turns, speeds slowed to 50 mph.

This 2nd annual Australian Grand Prix on Phillip Island was a cliff-hanger from the start with the lead changing hands 18 times during the course of the race. At the checkered flag, the name of the game, the winner was Gardner (**Honda**), with Doohan (**Honda**) and Rainey (**Yamaha**) finishing second and third respectively. For sports-crazed Aussies, the first Australian Grand Prix for motorcycles began on Phillip Island in April of 1989. But shortly thereafter, a major controversy erupted concerning cigarette advertising. So, after only two brief seasons, the Grand Prix was shifted to a new track at Eastern Creek, just west of Sydney in New South Wales (NSW).

Lord of the Bush

(Above) **A common sight** along the roadways of north-western Australia, the massive boab tree sheds its leaves during a "dry" further accentuating it's already witch-like appearance.

(Right) **Talcum-fine, red sand** underlies the heart of the Australian Outback.

(Far right) **A scarred and painted Djauan tribesman** sounds a haunting digerridoo.

The First Australians

Keepers of the Flame. In the Northern Territory of Australia, I came upon a group of painted Djauan aborigines carrying hard-wood spears and hunting boomerangs. Dressed for an evening "corroboree" (co-robbery), this storytelling dance dates back nearly 40,000 years to "Dreamtime," the complex aboriginal creation. When performed in the Outback centuries ago, the dancers decorated themselves with white ash from a smoldering fire and performed "au natural" in front of tribesmen. Living in two worlds today, the aboriginal dancers use white grease paint and wear tourist-pleasing breechcloths. During the encounter, I was forced to keep my helmet visor down to ward off the omnipresent Australian fly which infests "the bush" during the long, hot "dry."

FROM
BUCKINGHAM
PALACE
TO
THE GRAND PALACE
London to Bangkok

Modern-day knights in shining armor at
Bolsover Castle, Derbyshire, England,
prepare for medieval combat.

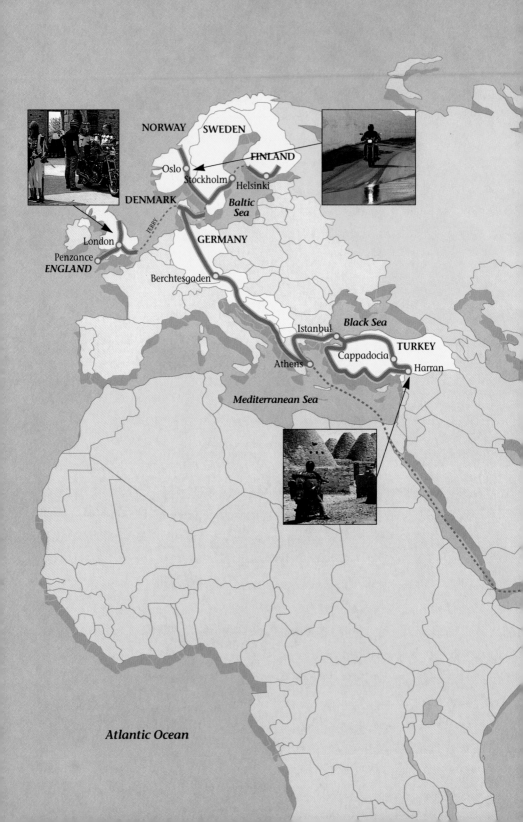

FROM
BUCKINGHAM PALACE
TO
THE GRAND PALACE

London to Bangkok

Chiang Mai

Bay of Bengal

Arabian Sea

South China Sea

Bangkok

Pattaya Beach

THAILAND

Gulf of Thailand

FREIGHTER

Georgetown

N

The ENDLESS RIDE

MALAYSIA

SINGAPORE

Indian Ocean

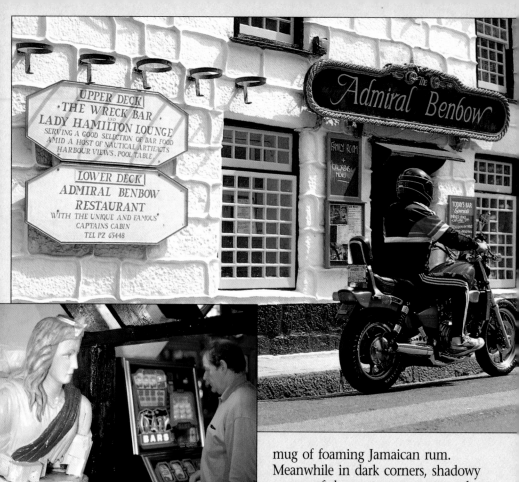

Smugglers, Wreckers, and Pirates

(Top) **At the seafaring port** of Penzance on the Cornish coast of Southern England, I visited the restored Admiral Benbow Inn. Once the haunt for the 18th century band of smugglers known as the "Benbow Brandy Men," this inn was to become world famous as the setting for the opening chapter of Robert Lewis Stevenson's novel "Treasure Island." Here, beneath a weathered thatched roof on cold, rainy, windswept nights, raucous gangs of bearded, scarred smugglers would gather to smoke "tabacky" or to down a

mug of foaming Jamaican rum. Meanwhile in dark corners, shadowy groups of desperate men met to plot future contraband "runs." The inn's greatest secret (known only to a handful of the most trusted patrons) lay buried beneath the structure: a secret tunnel which led from the waterwell in the courtyard to a secluded cove nearby. It was through this narrow opening, carved centuries earlier by Celtic "tinners," that the smugglers were able to escape after their bloody clashes with the King's revenue collectors.

(Left) **Inside the "Wreck Bar,"** a wistful figurehead, salvaged from a watery grave, watches in silence as a customer plays a game of chance. Open and without protection, the Cornish coast (that perilous doorstep to Britain) has claimed countless ships driven by gales or blinded by fog.

A pirate's haven. No port along the Cornish coast of England offered better protection to cut-throat pirates than Polruan and Fowey. Two garrisoned blockhouses guarded each side of the harbor entrance. As well, once the returning pirate fleet had passed safely through, a huge chain was lifted to deter pursuers. The narrow road descending to the small, colorful harbor at Polruan is one of the steepest on the Cornish coast.

Not a Straight Road in all of Cornwall

(Left) **As I rode along** the sunken coastal roads, over long-forgotten tunnels that once had connected remote farm houses to snug little coves, my mind flashed back to the 1750's, the Golden Age of Piracy. During a large "run," shadowy gangs of ruthless, bearded smugglers would overturn a wagon along this narrow lane, thereby rendering it impassable to the King's men. With the passing of time (and television), smuggling has become glamorized, even respectable. Today, many an inn along this wild Cornish coast displays signs reminiscent of that colorful era.

(Above) **Man has walked on this** southern tip of England for thousands of years. With each passing age, he has left his imprint upon the land. Built on a smaller scale than Stonehenge, the Quoits were erected nearly 4,000 years ago by the Celts. While some of the Quoits of Cornwall have undergone major rebuilding, this former burial chamber at Darite has remained virtually unchanged since the time of its construction.

ickingham Palace and the Changing of the Guard Ceremony are a "must see" ent for any rider visiting England. The palace, often described as "fit for a King," is been the official London residence of British monarchs since Queen Victoria as- nded the throne in 1837. The Changing of the Guard Ceremony is a daily event om April through July, and on alternate days throughout the remainder of the ar. On sunny days, the crowds are reminiscent of Super Bowl Sunday.

(Right) **A symbol of tradition** in a rapidly changing city, the mounted Life Guard regiment stands parade wearing bright red tunics and snow-white plumed helmets.

(Below) **The men of the Blues** and Royals regiment wear blue jackets with red-plumed helmets. By tradition, the Colonel-in-Chief of each regiment has been the reigning monarch – currently, Her Majesty Queen Elizabeth II.

(Far right) **Big Ben, London's favorite landmark,** rises nearly 330 feet above the Houses of Parliament. Pugilistic pubowner, Benjamin Caunts is believed by many to be the man whose name was affixed to the bell cast in 1856. However, that large bell cracked and shortly thereafter a second Big Ben weighing but 13 tons was cast as a replacement. This is the bell that you'll hear today, one that has chimed without fail since 1862.

Gateway to London. The Tower Bridge guards the river road to this historic city. Built between 1886 and 1894, the Gothic turrets were designed to blend with the nearby Tower of London. This bridge, over the glassy River Thames, is the only structure which can be raised to allow the passage of ships, although nowadays, openings are infrequent.

(Above) **Once within eyesight of the Tower Bridge**, historic Old London Bridge is now *the* tourist attraction of Lake Havasu, Arizona, in the great American Southwest. In 1962, when it was discovered that London Bridge was literally falling down, the British Government put the structure up for sale. The winning bid went to an American entrepreneur who had the bridge transported, stone by stone, to its present site. On October 10, 1971, it was officially reopened by the Lord Mayor of London.

(Left) **Yeoman Warders, or if you prefer,** Beefeaters have been a tradition at the Tower of London since the sixteenth century.

Guns and Roses

I've always been fascinated by weaponry — both medieval and modern — and, on my ride, I never missed a chance to see an unusual collection of arms nor to visit an historic battlefield.

(Below) **The Gallipoli Peninsula in Turkey.** The main Allied objective in the Gallipo Campaign of World War I was, by capturing Istanbul, to force Turkey out of the Wa It was to be a tragic miscalculation of Turkish resolve. Nine months after the initial landings, it was the Allied forces that were forced to withdraw, leaving behind 36,00 of their comrades. Turkish casualties were never revealed. A solitary fieldpiece today overlooks Anzac Cove, the scene of so much suffering.

Impregnable Jaigarh Fort, Jaipur, Rajasthan, India. The largest wheeled cannon ever built, the Jaya Vana, weighs 250 tons and was pulled by four adult elephants. The 20-foot-long barrel was cast from ten metals, including gold. The cannon was fired only once in its history, hurling a 110-pound cannon ball. The crude swastika, an Indian good luck sign, was painted on the barrel by the present day Maharaja of Jaipur, a failed art student.

The Imperial War Museum, London, England. In the rose garden are a pair of 15" naval guns, the most accurate cannons ever made. The near cannon came from the British battleship H.M.S. Ramillies while the far one was mounted on the H.M.S. Resolution. Both cannons saw service in the Sea of Marmara against Turkish shore installations. Only with the advent of the guided missile were these weapons relegated to history.

A Ride into Knighthood

One bright spring morning, I rode to Bolsover Castle, Derbyshire, England, to witness a colorful reenactment of medieval combat. As the crowds on this Bank Holiday weekend would be big, I arrived early so that I could leave my **Honda** within the castle walls.

(Top) **The Escafeld Medieval Society**, which organizes the elaborate event, does not use horses during combat. Rather, all jousting is done on foot. Nevertheless, the combat is so real and so full of emotion that an ambulance and nurses are always standing by as some of the knights get carried away. Literally!

(Above) **Riders visiting Bolsover Castle's Great Courtyard** are transported back to the days of knighthood and chivalry by the lavish use of brilliant tapestries, period costumes, and medieval weapons.

That was **then**...

...*This is* **now**

Compared with my state-of-the-art Arai helmet, the early 13th century headgear to the left and above were primitive in both design and manufacture. Padded with horsehair and lined with leather, the smell given off after a rainstorm must have been unforgettable! And, having no risible visor, the knights must have suffered from heat prostration on a hot summer afternoon. The Escafeld Medieval Society are such purists that they make all their own armor and weapons and so dedicated are the members to the authenticity of their replicas, they won't even consider using WD40 as a rust inhibitor!

Catching a small ferryboat
bound for Denmark, I
crossed the narrow sound
that separates Sweden from
Denmark and rode north to
visit historic Kronborg
castle at Elsinore.

p) **Kronborg castle has been well-known** for more than 400 years. To its foes,
onborg was the powerful fortress guarding the narrow body of water which separated
enmark from present day Sweden (at the time of the castle's construction, Denmark
ntrolled both shorelines). And to most seafaring men, Kronborg's battery of cannons
bove) enforced a very unpopular soundtoll on passing merchantmen. As an architectural
hievement, this festive Renaissance castle of copper-clad spires and towers, surrounded
 a stately moat, is one of the most acclaimed monuments in Europe. Constructed of
anic sandstone, the castle today is filled with woven tapestries and paintings dating back
 the 16th and 17th century. It was William Shakespeare, however, who immortalized the
stle by using it as the locale for his epic tragedy, "Hamlet."

The Tall Ships

(Left) **As I rode northward along** the west coast of Sweden, I stopped briefly at historic Gothenburg to visit the museum — home of the once mighty ocean-spanning sailing ships. Tattered entries in the log of "The Viking," a four-master in holiday dress, included voyages when she sailed as a grain carrier between Australia and her home port in Scandinavia and as a cadet ship for new Swedish midshipmen. More recently, the bark was outfitted and served as an exclusive supper club.

(Above) **Although connected by a new high** bridge to Sweden's west coast (just north of Gothenburg) small, rocky Smogen Island — gem of the North Sea jewel box — will always remain a Nordic yachtsman's hideaway.

(Above) **Summer in Helsinki, Finland**, is but a brief interlude between a welcome spring and the onslaught of winter. The only world capital farther north is Iceland's Reykjavik.

(Right) **Luxury Afloat.** The most lavish ferryboats anywhere in the world are those which ply the sea lanes between Sweden and Finland, and from Germany to Finland. Competition is so fierce on these summer runs that my **Honda** was transported **free of charge!** These floating pleasure palaces are equipped with the latest of creature comforts: multi-level restaurants, shopping malls, television lounges, multi-screen cinemas, game rooms, fashion boutiques, in-vogue discos, hairstyling salons, duty-free stores, and even saunas. Cruising the Baltic has come a long ways since the time of the spartan Viking longboat.

Verdant green hills and aging brown barns "hang up-side down" just north of Oslo, Norway.

Nordic Pagodas

(Far left and left) **Built in 1150,** the Stave Church of Borgund, Norway, is one of the oldest timbered structures in the world. Only this stave church — so named because of the enormous upright beams supporting it — and several others are the survivors of some 850 such churches built during the Middle Ages. The west portal bristles with dragon-decorated gables that resemble old Viking figureheads. These Nordic temples were erected with a specially treated hard pine in a process long since forgotten.

(Below) **In the Nordic High Country,** I rode past isolated log cabins built in a timeless style. Starting with a thin layer of birch bark, which served as a foundation, ranchers would stack on thick layers of roof sod. The purpose was to insulate the cabin against harsh winter conditions.

The lacy loveliness of the Seven Sisters Falls at Geiranger is without a doubt Norway's best known cataract. Its seven torrents of silver cascade 1,500 feet into the deep purple of a bottomless fjord. Ice-free the year round only because of the warm Gulf Stream, the glacial-scooped fjords serve as vital waterways between the interior regions of Norway and the busy sea lanes of the North Sea.

Filigrees of foam dissolve into mist with a deafening roar. In early summer countless lakes and massive glacial runoff flood every stream with chilly water.

...ding the fjordlands of
...estern Norway.
...nnually, around the first
... June, snowplows cut
...rough the winter
...alanches to open
...arrow, slippery, ice-walled
...ads which descend
...ecipitously to the iso-
...ted villages far below.

Autumn skies in the
Bavarian Alps are crisp and
cloudless with Mount
Watzmann, the snowcapped
landmark of southeastern
Germany, clearly visible from
the onion-domed church at
Maria Gern.

(Above) **Disoriented in the mountains**, I once stopped and asked a elderly innkeeper for directions to Berchtesgaden. "All roads lead downhill to Berchtesgaden," was his reply. At certain times of the year, this 29-degree slope must make for an interesting ride!

(Left) **After visiting the war memorial** in Berchtesgaden, I rode to nearby Obersalzberg to see what remained, if anything, of the Berghofs (chalets) that once belonged to Hitler and the Nazi hierarchy.

(Overleaf) **Every vestige of that era** has been erased, except for the Eagle's Nest. Built by Martin Bormann in 1938 and presented to Hitler on his 53rd birthday, the "tea house" (situated at 6,017 feet) miraculously survived destruction by both the Allies and the German post-war Governments. The view from the restaurant is spectacular! To visit the overlook, you'll have to leave your bike on the parking lot below and catch a packed tourist bus as the twisting four-mile switchback road has been closed to all private vehicles since 1952.

143

Sun-drenched walls encompass Adriatic Renaissance Treasures. Once the old port at Dubrovnik, Bosnia, guarded fleets of treasure-laden galleons; now pleasure craft prevail. This former city-state is the jewel of the Adriatic and few cities are more fragile or culturally richer.

(Left) **Late in the summer of** 1989, just prior to the outbreak of the Yugoslav civil war, I rode along the Dalmatian coast from Trieste in the north to Dubrovnik in the south. Renowned oceanographer Jacque Costeau once referred to this pristine coastline as the most beautiful in the world and a more picturesque ride would be hard to imagine. Sunset at Dubrovnik's embarkation wharf, found motorcycles queued for the twice-weekly sailing of the ferryboat to Greece. As the night was starlit and balmy and there was no indication of rain, I decided to save a few dollars by sleeping out on deck while enroute overnight to the Greek island of Corfu.

Right) **A view from the top** of ne medieval walls looking astward along Dubrovnik's main romenade reveals a Rome in iiniature, a Venice without canals.

Near the fabled Golden Horn of Istanbul, Turkey, the storied waterway that separates Europe from Asia, are the six pencil-thin minarets and the squat, bulbous dome belonging to the great imperial 17th century Blue Mosque. The color "blue" in the mosque's name is derived from the lavish use of azure tiles which decorate interior sections, most of which, unfortunately, are off-limits to non-believers.

I left Istanbul at dawn and rode all day across the hot, arid central region of Turkey to reach the "cone country" of Cappadocia. By some estimates, this belt around Göreme contains 50,000 cones. Some are tent size, others the size of minor skyscrapers. Long ago Mount Argaeus began the process of creating the cones by laying down a volcanic plateau. As the mass cooled, it cracked and, over the centuries, erosion did the rest. Turkish peasants, laboring like moles, have tunneled into the cones to create airy, low-cost living quarters.

(left) **It's only a half-hour ride** from Göreme to the primitive cave churches at
Ihlve. They were carved by the Monks who lived in this region from the 4th to the
14th centuries. As these caverns are windowless, they're confining. If you suffer
from claustrophobia, wait until the last tourist bus leaves, so that once inside, you
can move about freely to examine the frescoed walls.

(above) **Rows of solar roof panels** add a modern touch to this rock-hewn cave-
home. Although I camped outdoors in Göreme, there's a mystique about this valley
that attracts even the first-time visitor into spending a night in a cave. As a
result, you'll discover that nearly all the smaller hotels are nothing more than
modified caves.

The Ride that Failed

Twice in late August, I tried to ride up 7,100 foot Mount Nemrut Dagi, a remote mountain in Central Turkey. On both attempts I was unsuccessful. As the road was under repair, I was forced to stay in low gear. With the air temperature hovering around 115 °F, my temperature gauge quickly hit the redline. But, as I had ridden thousands of miles to reach this remote site, I didn't want to leave empty-handed. So, one morning, I joined a group of young Turkish students and in a Jeep bumped my way to the top. Turkey is criss-crossed with earthquake faults. As a result, when the enormous stone heads atop 7,100 foot Mount Nemrut Dagi were discovered in 1881, they were scattered like tenpins. Today, erected upright and arranged with some semblance of order, this archeological site is a popular hiking destination.

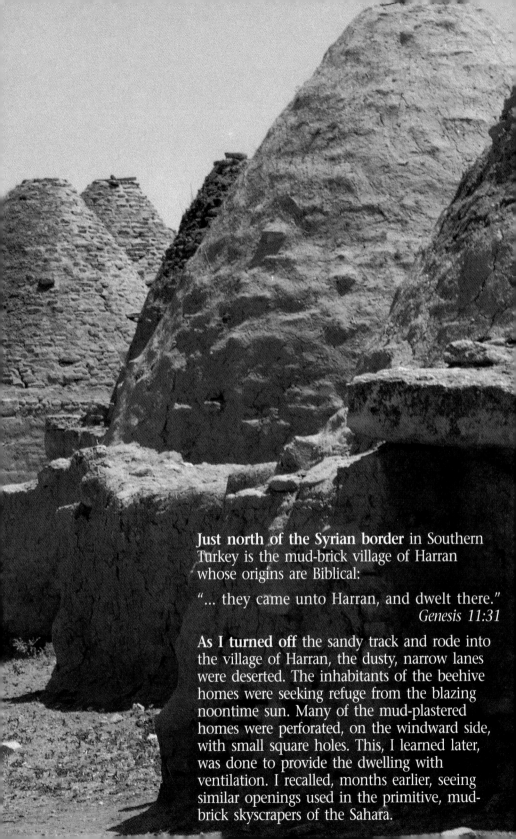

Just north of the Syrian border in Southern
Turkey is the mud-brick village of Harran
whose origins are Biblical:

"... they came unto Harran, and dwelt there."
Genesis 11:31

As I turned off the sandy track and rode into
the village of Harran, the dusty, narrow lanes
were deserted. The inhabitants of the beehive
homes were seeking refuge from the blazing
noontime sun. Many of the mud-plastered
homes were perforated, on the windward side,
with small square holes. This, I learned later,
was done to provide the dwelling with
ventilation. I recalled, months earlier, seeing
similar openings used in the primitive, mud-
brick skyscrapers of the Sahara.

No Sense of Humor!

I'd been in Singapore about 10 days when, one afternoon, I was stopped in the Orchard Road/Scott Road tourist mecca by two motorcycle policemen.

"Sir, since 1975 its been against the law to wear a full-faced helmet" (seems that bandits used to wear them whenever they robbed a gold store).

"It's an even greater offense," added the second officer, "to wear a smoked visor" (evidently only bank robbers wear them).

"No problem, fellas, I've got another helmet," and with that I reached into my pack and pulled out a photograph of myself taken a week earlier wearing a lion mask. The story behind the lion mask is as follows:

Multiracial Singapore is predominantly Chinese and no Asian business man would ever think of opening a new enterprise without hiring a group of lion dancers to ward off the evil spirits.

Earlier in the week, as I watched the Chin Woo Dance Group pack their costumes for an upcoming performance, on impulse, I suddenly picked up a lion mask, placed it over my head, sat on my **Honda** and took a self-portrait.

The young Chinese school kids, who had gathered to watch, roared with laughter.

The Singapore Police didn't even crack a smile!

"Sir, you have until tomorrow to comply," and with that, they disappeared in a cloud of blue smoke.

That evening, over a cold beer at Brannigan's Pub, I considered my options. If I stayed in Singapore, I was going to have to buy a second helmet. If I left, I could save $40.

At dawn the next morning, I rode across the narrow causeway that separated Singapore Island from the mainland of Southeast Asia and entered the steaming jungle world of Malaysia.

Note: On April 1, 1993, it became legal to wear a full-faced helmet in the island-state. And a smoked visor? Today in Singapore, only someone making a large withdrawal from a bank (at gunpoint) would wear one!

(Right) **Often referred to as** the cleanest city in Southeast Asia, Singapore maintains that reputation with draconian fines for minor infractions: $500 for dropping chewing gum on the sidewalk. In an era of unchecked graffiti, Singapore has the answer!

Everyone's favorite Chinese City

(Left) **Founded in 1786,** the city of Georgetown (on Penang Island off the west coast of Malaysia) is the oldest former British colony in Southeast Asia, even predating Singapore.

(Above) **Malaysia, like neighboring Thailand** and Indonesia, is the Asian home of the **Honda** 100 cc. motorbike. With restrictions on motorcycles having an engine capacity over 150 cc., only the very wealthy can afford a bike having an import duty up to 400 percent of the purchase price.

163

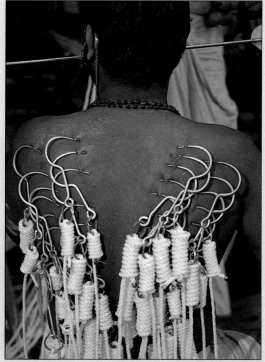

The Coming of Dawn

Early light at Georgetown on Penang Island, reveals large groups of religious zealots, dressed in brilliant yellow robes which are symbolic of the annual Indian Thaipusam Festival. Each Hindu follower is in a trance-like state achieved after days of fasting and meditation. Some of the male participants pierce their cheeks and tongues with fine silver spears while others skewer themselves with hooks, later to be used for pulling the Chariot of the Gods. Amazing as it may seem, throughout the pilgrimage, I never once noticed a single drop of blood being spilt nor any indication of pain being felt by the zealots.

165

(Far left and left) **The Royal Mosque of Perak** is in Kuala Kangsar on the west coast of Malaysia. Commonly known as the Ubadiah Mosque, the unique onion-domed roof and compressed minarets give the illusion that one is seeing it through a distorted mirror.

(Below) **The former Royal Palace** of the Sultan of Perak, now a museum, was built at the turn of the century without the use of a single nail.

(Above) **The *Pomerai*, Thailand's** goodluck garland.

(Right) **I had been riding in Thailand** for only a few hours when an oncoming bus swerved into my lane and forced me off the road. When it happened again a few days later, I decided to seek help. A Thai friend suggested that I buy several *pomerais* and present them as gifts to the massive Golden Buddha overlooking Pattaya Beach. The ride up to the location was uneventful; on my return trip, however, I was again chased off the road, this time by a truck. I knew then that I was going to have to seek further assistance or else I'd be leaving Thailand in a wooden box.

(Left) **West of the old capital** of Chiang Mai, the "Rose of the North," I rode through Wat Suan Dok, a temple complex built for the nobles of Thailand (wat means temple). Buddhist Temples in the Kingdom serve many functions: as gathering places for celebrations, as asylums for meditation, as orphanages for the young, and more recently, as drug rehabilitation centers.

(Above) **I rode to Nakhon Sawan** to see an English friend married to a Thai girl. After hearing of my narrow escapes, Bernie suggested that I get my **Honda** blessed by the saffron-robed Buddhist monks.

171

Buddha Policy

The **solemn ceremony began** with the recital of a prayer in Pali, an ancient language that rivals Sanskrit in its origin. Then, using a water-soluble white paint, the abbot painted nine white circles (the perfect number) on my **Honda**. Reaching for a bowl filled with Holy water, he began to circle my **Honda**. As he circled, so he splashed and every time he passed me, I got hit! After what seemed an eternity of dousing, the "well" finally ran dry! My **Honda** Magna 700 was blessed in Nakhon Sawan (Sawan in Thai means Heaven). Now I felt doubly insured, having my **Honda** blessed and in Heaven to boot!

(Below and right) **Revered by Buddhist monks**, the soaring golden Chedi dominates the skyline of the Grand Palace, Bangkok's foremost attraction.

Mirrored Dragons, Golden *Chofas* and Man-Bird *Garudas* Adorn the Grand Palace

(Middle left) **A giant, mythological Yak** stands sentry while a toothy, hand-crafted, glass-mosaic demon *(above)* upholds an ornate spire outside the Pantheon.

(Left) **As I rode along the narrow pathways** that encompassed the Grand Palace — pathways where once royal Siamese elephants paraded — I forgot about Bangkok's notorious traffic jams, its pollution, its sticky, high humidity, and its summertime floods. There was something magical about this Grand Palace that seemed to cast a veil over the harsh reality of everyday city life.

Rising above the deserted parade ground, the golden Chedi and Prangs of the Grand Palace gleam in the setting tropical sun.

"The Bridge on the River Kwai"

Nearly half a century has passed since the infamous "Death Railway" was operational, but countless visitors still travel to Kanchanaburi, Thailand, to see the bridge immortalized by Pierre Boulle in his epic novel "The Bridge on the River Kwai." The railway carried military supplies to the Japanese forces fighting in Burma until February 13, 1945, when Allied bombers knocked out two of the center spans. The arched, steel girder next to the left concrete pier is one of the original bridge spans, while the angular ones to the right are the replacement sections.

(Far left and left) **Situated 78 miles west of Bangkok,** the bridge and the "Death Railway" were completed and maintained at an appalling cost in human lives. Estimates run as high as 16,000 Allied POWs and perhaps 100,000 Asian laborers died here. As I walked between the well-groomed rows of bronze headstones, I noticed that most of those buried here died in their early twenties. Known as the JEATH Cemetery, it contains not only the graves of Allied soldiers but also Japanese soldiers who fell in combat.

(Below left) **An unexploded, 1,000-pound** bomb dwarfs my **Honda.** During the Allied air raid, two bombs failed to explode on contact. Following the war, they were fished from the river, defused and today stand as silent sentinels guarding this Bridge of Sorrow.

Near the Golden Triangle of Thailand, where fields of poppies (opium) were once the only cash crop, I met two Akha hilltribe girls wearing traditional costumes. Focusing through the viewfinder, I suddenly noticed one of the girls throwing up her hand signalizing STOP! Then, as I looked on in amazement, she leaned over, grabbed one of my mirrors and began to primp her hairdo. All girls are cut from the same bolt of cloth!

(Left) **"Indiana Jones" would have loved this place!** Joined to Bangkok by an all-weather road, Ayutthaya, the former capital, is Thailand's archetypical lost-city-in-the-jungle. At Wat Phraram, I was engulfed in a tide of lush vegetation swirling around the decaying prangs.

(Above) **Decapitated Buddhas** were everywhere, some beheaded by war, others stolen for the illicit art market.

185

Hands Across the Centuries. The ancient Buddhist temple at Sukhothai, a five-hour ride north of Bangkok, surrounds a massive 50-foot, seated Buddha. Throughout the day I watched as villagers came to pay their respect with acts of devotion, seeking favor for some wish they wanted to be granted — like the winning numbers of the national lottery!

The "Bird" encounter. One day at Pattaya Beach, I rode out to see Father Brennan, the priest in charge of the orphanage. On entering the grounds, I saw a pretty young girl named Bird practicing the Thai classic dance. As I started to enter the chapel, she asked, "Will you give me a ride before you leave?" "Sure, but you've got to wear a helmet." When I came out an hour later, there was Bird grasping my **Honda**, wearing her "helmet." "What am I going to do?" "Take her for a ride," Father Brennan replied. So with Bird riding the buddy seat, we rode around the grounds while the other kids roared their approval. I think it made her day, I know it made mine.

(Right) **A Pair of Magnas.** I left Pattaya Beach with a friend to see the new temple complex located about half-an-hour's ride to the south. Intricately sculptured, Chinese dragons are far more detailed and impressive than are their Thai counterparts. As this complex had just been finished, the colors of the dragons were dazzling.

(Below) **As I rode through the ornate gates**, I was impressed by the extent of the temple. Flanking the entryway to the main building were a pair of 15-ton, pink-granite, Beijing lions that had been sent to the King of Thailand as a gift from the People's Republic of China.

A Thai mystery unraveled. Pattaya Beach, Thailand, was the only city I visited where large cc. motorcycles were readily available for rent. With a law against the importation of anything over 150 cc., I was curious to know how these bikes got into the Kingdom. One afternoon, I asked "Suzy," a pretty Thai girl, if she could fill me in.

The motorcycles I saw for rent, she explained, had been "run out" worldwide. They had then been shipped to Japan where, in small mom and pop workshops, they had been remanufactured before being crated and exported to Thailand as parts (there are no cc. restrictions on "parts" entering the Kingdom). On arrival, the parts were reassembled in backrooms, with many of the reborn motorcycles then being sold as "new." This scam, she told me, was only used with large motorcycles and not with the omnipresent 100 cc. motorbikes that dominate the Thai scene.

Thailand is one of the least expensive countries in Southeast Asia in which to live and is a rider's delight. For example, you can rent this 1987 CBR for a mere $12 a day, or "with Suzy" for $32 a day.

189

Inflation in Paradise

(Left) **Northeast of Malaysia lies** a cluster of small islands with swaying coconut palms and white sandy beaches, washed by the warm waters of the South China Sea. Koh Samui (Samui Island) is Thailand's third largest island. In 1975, when I first visited, it was not even on the tourist map. In those days, I rented a palm-frond beach shack on tropical Chaweng Beach for 50 Baht ($2) a night. Eighteen years later, when I returned with my **Honda**, the rental price of a palm-frond shack had skyrocketed to an unbelievable $4 a night. I didn't know if I could afford it!

(Above) **Once coconuts and copra were** the main cash crop of Koh Samui. Now tourism prevails.

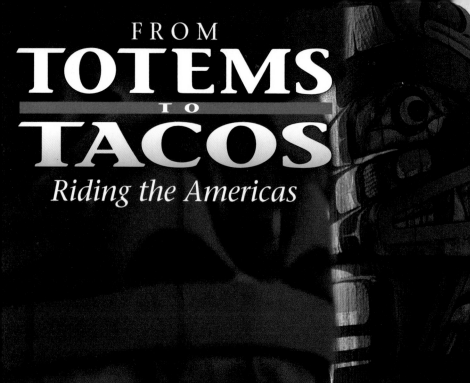

FROM
TOTEMS
TO
TACOS
Riding the Americas

Golden Age of Totems. From 1850 to 1900, totem poles were the principal means of preserving the history of the Indians of the Pacific Northwest. A revival of this ancient art-form flourishes today in the City of Duncan on Vancouver Island (off the west coast of Canada) where 37 carved totems are on display.

FROM

TOTEMS

TO

TACOS

Riding the Americas

Hudson Bay

CANADA

Dawson Creek

Alaska

Fairbanks

Yukon Territory

ALCAN HIGHWAY

Watson Lake

British Columbia

Mount McKinley

Anchorage

Vancouver Island

Riding the Gold Trail

"There's gold, and it's haunting and haunting;

It's luring me on as of old;

Yet it isn't the gold that I'm wanting

So much as just finding the gold."

— Robert Service

The discovery of gold along the banks of the American River in 1848 triggered one of the most frenzied migrations in human history — The California Gold Rush.

(Right) **It's an easy, four-hour ride** east from San Francisco to historic Columbia, tucked away in the low foothills of the Mother Lode country. Columbia is probably the best preserved gold mining town in California. Beneath its "theme park" veneer, it offers so much historical authenticity that it's the nearest thing to stepping back in time.

(Far right) **The largest gold nugget** ever found in the Mother Lode country was discovered near Carson Hill, eight miles north of Columbia. The nugget is said to have weighed 196 pounds!

It may have been that discovery in 1850 that today draws "prospectors" of all ages to try their luck at panning for gold.

ft) **Though prone to robbery by** **ghwaymen**, Wells Fargo began an press stagecoach service in Columbia the 1850's to carry passengers and old dust" between the booming shan- towns of Copperopolis, Poverty Hill, uabbletown, etc. By 1870, after 2.5 llion ounces of the precious yellow etal had been extracted, Columbia's rtunes began to fade. Today, the old gecoach serves to haul tourists to the

many "diggin's" around town as the "greenback" has long since replaced the "dust" of yesteryear.

(Above) **Harvesting the wind.** Since the beginning of time, man has looked for alternative sources of energy. In the Altamont Pass area, about an hour east of San Francisco, you'll ride through one of the largest accumulation of wind generators in the world.

(*Above*) **Early one morning**, with low shards of sunlight piercing the darkness, I turned off the main route along northern California's wild and rugged coast and followed the road signs to Humboldt State Park and the Redwood Groves known as "Avenue of the Giants."

(*Right*) **The Roots of Heaven.** As if to embrace the sky, coastal redwoods soar 350 feet or more and many acquire an age well over 2,000 years. Pausing for a moment along the shoulder, all was silent except for the creaking of some massive branches stirring dozens of stories above me.

Born of Fire and Ice

Like vying photographers striving for an impossible view, the wind and the light are constantly changing the perspective of snow-capped, volcanic Crater Lake (located in the Cascade Range of southern Oregon in the western part of the United States). Mirror-like under zero wind conditions, it's 6-miles across from rim to rim. Blanketed by snow, the mountainous road at 6,000 feet was chilly in the early morning and, as a result, I was wearing my Dri-Rider to ward off the penetrating cold.

The world's largest totem (in diameter) is the Cedar Man in Duncan, on Vancouver Island, British Columbia, Canada. It's 7 feet in diameter, 24 feet high and is carved from a western red cedar.

bove) **Like an obelisk of ancient Egypt**, totem is carved in a horizontal position. sing only a knife, a short handled ax, and a iisel, the early Indian craftsmen of the Pacific orthwest were inspired by religious impulses, bal rituals, and legendary characters. But that as then, this is now. As I watched a young ' shirt-clad-artist begin a new totem, the und of blaring rock music was intermixed ith the high-pitched scream of a chain saw. f my ancestors had owned a chain saw," he id, "they would have used it."

ight) **The smallest totem pole** I came across as in the gold rush boomtown of Skagway, laska. Note the worn wooden sidewalks, a mnant of the historic stampede era.

(Left) **A grinning bear greets my Honda** Magna 700. This carved 20-foot pole at the University of Alaska in Fairbanks was originally painted in only black (from charcoal) and red (from berries). The carved animals depicted on totems are not gods nor demons and were never worshipped, nor was there ever any satanic reference implied.

(Left and above) **The animals most often found** decorating a pole are the whale and the wolf. Legend has it that *whales*, rubbing against certain offshore rocks, could change themselves into *wolves* and thereby hunt on land. Other animals used by the carvers are: the *beaver*, personifying hard work; the *eagle*, Chief of the Sky Beings; *seals*, believed to be in touch with both the spirit and real world; and *frogs*, symbolic of wisdom.

GISBORNE
NEW ZEALAND
first City of the Sun
8248 MILES
GISBORNE HOST LIONS

Signpost Forest

At isolated **Watson Lake**, Milepost 592 in the Yukon Territory, the signposts may have had a happen-stance origin, but those days have long since passed. Today, hand carried signs *(above)* from the far corners of the world, some being nothing short of works of art, are erected by adventurers heading northward to Alaska, America's last frontier.

DAWSON
CREEK

FT ST. JOHN 48
FORT NELSON 300
WHITEHORSE 918
FAIRBANKS 1523

MILE
"O"

MILE
"O"

A
L
A
S
K
A
H

A
L
A
S
K
A
H

The Alcan Highway
(Alaska Highway), built
during the second world
war, was the engineering
marvel of its time. Con-
structed in just 9 months
during 1942, it was originally 1,671 miles in length.
But with the straightening o
the curves (rumor had it
they were deliberately
designed into the road to

nfuse Japanese bombers
ho might try to attack
nerican truck convoys),
e highway now
etches just 1,523 miles.
ilepost "0" begins in
nada at Dawson Creek,
itish Columbia, *(Left)*
d extends to Milepost
523 in Fairbanks, Alaska.
nis is an equivalent
ling distance of going

from sweltering
Casablanca, Morocco to
icy Oslo, Norway.

(Right) **A wall mural at
Whitehorse**, capital of
Canada's Yukon Territory,
depicts the construction
of the Alcan Highway as
an unending battle
between man and the
relentless forces of nature.

Panoramic views along the Alcan Highway range from mud to the magnificent. With "frost heaves" a common roadway occurrence, you'll find that the highway is in a never-ending-state of repair.

n old sternwheeler speaks out of st glories at Whitehorse on the ikon River. Restored to its original ndition, the S. S. Klondike mains today as the sole survivor 250 great ships that serviced the 398 Klondike Gold Rush. Mea- uring 210 feet in length and 42 et in width, this timber-burning essel took a day and a half to ddle down-river from Whitehorse Dawson, "The City of Gold."

213

On Whose Weathered Decks
Jack London Once Strolled

For almost nine decades, the stern-wheeler was the mainstay of the Yukon transportation system. They were first introduced into the lower Yukon River from the Bering Sea in 1866. With the Gold Rush of '98, it was the upper river, between Whitehorse and Dawson, that saw the heavy traffic. During the Stampede, travel onboard was fraught with danger, some man made, some natural. To the lively tune of banjo music, cancan girls and shady riverboat gamblers rubbed elbows with sourdough miners. Danger was omnipresent at every bend in the river where white-water rapids awaited their next careless pilot. Built in 1936 to the same specifications as her forerunners, the S. S. Klondike served briefly as a cargo

uler before her short, colorful career
me to a sudden end with the opening
the all weather road. In a last ditch
tempt to save her, she was completely
furbished and scheduled to serve as a
uise ship. But that idea was at least
irty years ahead of its time as tourists
d yet to discover "The Spell of the
ikon." In August of 1955, traveling

under full power, the S. S. Klondike
steamed into Whitehorse on her last run.
With flags flying and bands playing, she
was turned over to the Canadian government to serve as a historic remembrance.
Her enshrinement marked the end of a
romantic era which saw the sternwheeler
as an adventuresome symbol of travel in
the frozen Far North.

(*Above*) **Much pain, little gain.** In this early 1898 photograph, the Klondike stampeders of yesteryear can be seen streaming like ants in an almost unbroken line, climbing the icy steps to the summit of the Chilkoot Pass. Their ultimate destination was the Klondike River at Dawson, hence the name, the Klondike Stampede.

(*Right*) **A Fountain of Glaciers.** In the late 1960's, Marion and I photographed and produced "Flying Alaska," a documentary/adventure film about flying in the frozen Far North. From that motion picture film, the Chedalothna Glacier is seen beneath our wings being joined by tributary glaciers, adding stripes of moraine debris while giving the resultant glacier the appearance of a super highway. Due to the near continual cloud coverage over Mount McKinley (called "Denali" or the "Great One" by the Indians) and the lack of access roads to the glacial face, your best chance of seeing this phenomena of nature is from the air.

A Raped Wilderness

In Alaska, not all the gold was found on the surface as nuggets. Some lay under 200 feet of frozen ground. An hour's ride north of Fairbanks will take you to the placer mining area, a devastated, boulder-strewn wasteland created by the tailings from the gigantic, gold-ore dredges. Between the years 1924-1964, the miners took what they wanted and left without a conscience.

(Below) **In Fairbanks,** yesteryear's 6-cubic-foot ore buckets are today's planter boxes.

(Top) **Boomtown Prices.** During the stampede of '98, miners arriving in Skagway carried a mooseskin poke (a pouch) and paid their way in raw gold. A slice of bread in those days cost $1 and a dollar was measured by the amount of "gold dust" that you could place between your thumb and your forefinger (like a pinch). Little has changed over the years! The cost of a ferryboat ticket for me and my **Honda** Magna 700 from Skagway, Alaska, to Bellingham, Washington, was $407 (like a fistful of gold) and the meals onboard were extra!

(Right) **The terminus for the "Inside Passage,"** the inland waterway that extends from the United States to Alaska, is the former gold rush boomtown at Skagway. In the days of '98, it was a ritual for the arriving ship's crew to decorate the harbor rocks with their ship's name or that of their senior officer. It's a custom that still prevails today

(Right) **An old narrow gauge steam locomotive** from the White Pass & Yukon Railroad (known locally as the "Wait Patiently and You'll Ride" Railroad) meets all incoming cruise ships to transports sightseers to the summit of scenic White Pass.

Monument Valley

In the cold, copper light of dawn, I left my tent at the Mitten campground and rode to the road's end to admire the great stone monuments that straddle the Arizona-Utah border in the heart of the Navajo country in the great American Southwest.

Where once hostile Indians roamed. Hollywood's motion picture industry discovered Monument Valley in 1938. It was the setting for the award-winning western film, "Stagecoach," staring John Wayne. Since that time, dozens of films have been made here using the magnificent monuments of this Navajo Parkland as a backdrop.

Wearing his wealth in turquoise and silver, a Navajo cowboy awaits a hire as a park guide. More than 400,000 visitors arrive annually to explore this Navajo Tribal Park.

Unless you're riding a dirt bike and can handle deep, soft sand, scorching temperatures, and unfamiliar terrain, it's best to leave your motorcycle at the Visitors Center and take a four hour, 4-wheeled Navajo-guided-tour of the valley floor.

(Above) **Sculptured by centuries of erosion**, the Totem Pole on the right and the Yei Bi Chai on the left are best seen at sunset when long, dark fingers of shadow stretch silently across the rippled, eolian sand.

urnished by the wind and the rain over
e millennia, the Sun's Eye *(Above right)*
d the Ear of the Wind *(Right)*, located in
idden Valley, a remote corner of
onument Valley, are sacred sites to
dians of the Navajo Nation.

Rising Like Prehistoric Sentinels

The "Ayers Rock" of the American Southwest. Rising above a darkening valley floor, the West Mitten and the East Mitten emit an eerie glow at sunset, reminiscent of Australia's greatest Outback attraction.

Soaring on the
Winds of Adventure

The Kodak International Balloon Fiesta
Albuquerque, New Mexico

When Polar Bears Fly

Hailed as "the Sport of Gods," hot-air ballooning has withstood the winds of change. The Kodak International Balloon Fiesta is the largest gathering of balloon aficionados in the world. In 1994, 670 entries from 81 countries celebrated this uplifting sport. Today's balloons are a far

y from the primitive airship used by the ontgolfier brothers in the 1780's. Then, ylon was an unknown entity and the el burned was derived from a vile ixture of sulfurous coal and wool. 'hen blown off course, many an airborne dventurer was greeted by terrified, pitch-fork-wielding farmers upon landing! Today's balloon bags, or envelopes, are sewn of lightweight, ripstop nylon fabrics. Borne aloft by lift provided from clean-burning propane gas, these multicolored orbs are a pageant of visual poetry when wave after wave arise en masse.

233

Highlight of the week-long Fiesta, held annually during the first week of October, is the special shape balloons. This event offers commercial sponsors an opportunity to "air" their wares. *(Right)* This whimsical entry, a "Canine with Pups," stole the show!

Note: More than a million spectators attend this event yearly. As a result, motel rooms are impossible to get! I'd recommend staying at the nearby KOA campground east of Albuquerque as its convenient, clean, inexpensive and there are always lots of other bikers in attendance.

As Lonely as the Sahara

Heading southward through the great **Sonora Desert** of Northern Mexico, I rode my **Honda** for hours without seeing another vehicle. Although it was February and the peak of the tourist season, the Indian uprising during 1994 in the southern state of Chiapas appeared to be having a devastating effect upon tourism.

(Right) If *topes* (man-made speed-bumps) are the curse of riding through Mexican towns, then the *vado,* or ford, is the ever-present danger of desert riding. Warnings signs during the *Chubasco* (hurricane) season must be heeded as flash-floods occur with alarming suddenness.

The pyramids of **Egypt** and Yucatán — a world of difference, half a world apart. Egyptian pyramids *(Below)* were essentially the tombs of the pharaohs while Maya pyramids *(Right)* served as temple foundations. Hence, the ones you'll see today in Mexico are flat-topped. As I climbed the 91 time-worn steps to the top of El Castillo at Chichén Itzá, Yucatán, my Maya guide warned, "Don't look down."

Although small in stature, the Maya were a tough, warlike race with a passion for sports. Taken back from the jungle at Chichén Itzá are several ball courts *(Above and far right)*, the largest being 490 feet by 110 feet with walls reaching nearly 30 feet in height. On Maya "Super Bowl Sunday," magnificently dressed teams such as the "Chichén *Jaguars*" and the "Maya *Eagles*" played a game that resembled a cross between modern day soccer and basketball (note the stone hoop turned on its side). Using only their elbows, knees, and hips, they played as though their very lives depended upon the outcome, for indeed they did. With the winning goal, the champions would cut off the heads of the losers and this of course made everyone try a little harder.

(Right) **Mute skulls in stone testify** to the Maya custom of human sacrifice.

eft) **Freed from the green grasp** of the ingle, the unrestored Hall of a Thousand olumns and the Temple of the Warriors e surrounded by a hostile environment. akes lurk in the tall grass while ticks fest the foliage. Sunset brings out ordes of ferocious mosquitoes. While imping at the nearby Pyramid Inn, I ade it a daily practice to shake out my oes in the morning, looking for scorpins, before putting them on.

(Above) **Out of the pages of mystery** they came and for nearly fifteen centuries the Maya society flourished in the remote reaches of the Yucatán Peninsula and Central America. The collapse of their expansive civilization was as sudden as its unexplained arrival. Whole metropolises were abandoned; the entire population vanished and the thick green walls of the jungle engulfed their once mighty monuments.

ft) **In Acapulco, I was camped** at the ya Suave Trailer Park (across the street m Hornos Beach) where I met Bob stra, a Harley dealer from a small town Iowa. He had just ridden 3,000 miles his 1990 Harley-Davidson Heritage tail Classic. As he enjoyed snorkeling, spent many an afternoon exploring fs surrounding the bay.

(Above) **Once, socially conscious Acapulco,** on the west coast of Mexico, had a morning beach (Caleta) and an afternoon beach (Hornos). But over the years much of that snobbery has worn off and today Hornos is a laid-back beach where, over a leisurely cup of coffee, you can watch the daily coming and going of the cruise ships.

Acapulco's newest resorts are spread out along the beach road enroute to the airport. The posh Mayan Palace, with its soaring *palapas* (palm-thatched roofs), and the Acapulco Princess, with its tropical jungle waterfalls, over look pristine Revolcadero Beach

A Moorish Enclave
Las Hadas, Manzanillo, Mexico

An eight hour ride north of Acapulco will take you to Manzanillo and Las Hadas, an architectural fantasy world of mosque-like spires and domes, magic white towers, and marble-lined paths and cupolas. The resort, a Moorish inspiration built by Bolivian tin baron Patiño, took 12 years to construct at a cost of 33 million dollars. In March of 1974, 300 "beautiful people" from the jet set attended the "Gala in White" inauguration party. They stayed but a week and left, seeking yet another Xanadu.

Faced with rising costs and an empty 220-room resort on the isolated west coast of Mexico was bad enough, but fate was to deal Patiño yet another blow. The 1970's saw the beginning of the Gay Rights movement and owning a hotel with the name Las Hadas (the Fairies) was not exactly what Patiño intended. Ultimately, Las Hadas was sold to its present owner, the Camino Real chain of hotels.

Las Hadas is an enchanting mirage that one might imagine could only be found in a dream. Don't miss it when you're riding through.

Devil's Marbles

(Right) **Once the sphere of missionaries,** soldiers and miners, Baja California's wilderness, today, appeals to adventurous riders, drawn by the mystique of exploring a foreign land. Although the trans-peninsula highway was paved in 1973, it still has potholes, dips, and washes. And you'll soon discover that you never really ride this road, you endure it.

(Below) **Surviving Emblem of Baja's Wilds.** Near Punta Prieta, halfway to the Cape, I paused under the shade of a giant cardón cactus. The cactus family of plants distinguishes Baja's desert flora from that of the Sahara of North Africa, the Nubian Desert of Egypt, the Negev of Israel, the Thar Desert of Western India, and the Great Western Desert of Australia. Many of the plants found growing in this gnarled finger of land appear nowhere else on earth.

(Above) **While most of the adobe missions** of Baja lie in ruins, the stone mission on the cacti-covered slope at Mulegé still holds regular masses, just as it has for the last 300 years.

(Right) **The mission trail.** Situated in a vast depression, adjacent to where an underground river springs forth, is the oasis at Mulegé. During the 18th century, Jesuit Priests built a mission and planted the date palms that you'll find today.

At **El Coyote Bay**, a twin palm, encompassed by a pristine beach, issues an invitation to a sea of dreams. Riding my **Honda** Magna 700 southward from Tijuana to Guerro Negro (halfway down Baja), I was continually shrouded in a cold, grey mist. However, once I headed eastward across the Vizcaino Desert, the weather became quite summer-like. For a week I rode along the cacti-covered shoreline of Conception Bay, stopping at secluded coves to snorkel in crystal-clear waters or to sleep-out under the stars.

Slice of Heaven

(Left) **During the 1960's,** I flew to Baja's isolated Cape to enjoy the spectacular marlin fishing. Then, large sea turtles were a common sight, as were scallops — some 10 inches across.

(Above) **Today, renowned Hotel Cabo San Lucas,** located on lovely Chileno Bay at Baja's southern tip, still serves up lobster, folklore, and tranquillity. "I recommend the female lobster," suggested Guillermo, the maître d', "as its tail is larger and the meat is sweeter."

eft) **Old timers at the Cape** continually remi-
sce about the rustic fish cannery of the '30's
d the provincial charm that was once Cabo
n Lucas. Sadly, those days are gone forever.
day, the new "Cabo look" is one of cruise
ips, lavish hotels, and soaring condominiums.

bove) **Once a haven for pirates**, Cabo San
cas has sheathed its 18th century cutlasses in
vor of 20th century fishing poles. More than
0 species of fish abound at this confluence of
e Sea of Cortés and the Pacific Ocean,
aking it one of North America's richest
hing grounds.

Sculptured by the incessant pounding of the surf, the timeless arch at Lands' End is the true tip of the Baja Peninsula. This view is taken looking westward toward the Pacific Ocean.

Sunrise lights up a wandering life-style. Now, after an odyssey of more than five years that took me to 51 foreign lands, my ride was coming to an end. As I watched the first rays of dawn light the eastern sky over the Sea of Cortés, I wondered what the future had in store. Would there be other rides, other countries to visit, other adventures?

For those who have savored the seduction of international riding, Robert Service in his poem "Spell of the Yukon" answers that question.

"...
There are hardships that
nobody reckons;
There are valleys unpeopled
and still;
There's a land — oh, it
beckons and beckons,
And I want to go back —
and I will."

The ENDLESS RIDE

Notes

The 19-Language Parts & Service Phrasebook

Whenever you cross an international frontier into a different language zone, you can obtain fast, friendly motorcycle service by using this new, 19-language *Parts and Service Phrasebook*. There are no tongue-twisting phonetics to mispronounce;

simply show the page and point to the numbered phrase. Nothing could be easier!

This new, exclusive 19-language *Parts and Service Phrasebook* was compiled with the cooperation of 20 leading Honda distributors that I met on my worldwide ride.

AT THE REFUELING STATION

1. Do you have 95 octane, leaded or 4-Star?
2. Super?
3. Unleaded?
4. Is this the main road to __ ?
5. Will this road go to __ ?
6. To the left
7. Straight ahead
8. To the right
9. Behind
10. Is there a motorcycle repair shop near here?
11. About how many kilometers to __ ?

PARTS & SERVICE

12. I have a dead battery. Do you have jumper cables/jump leads?
13. The Positive (+) Terminal
14. The Negative (-) Terminal
15. Can you charge my battery?
16. Can you please give me a push start/bump start?
17. Do you have distilled water?
18. Do you have a new battery?
19. Can you adjust my valves? My intake is __ , my exhaust is __ .
20. Do you have shims?
21. The engine won't start. Can you check-out the problem?
22. The engine is running rough. Can you check-out the problem?
23. I have an unusual sound in the engine.
    Can you check-out the problem?

YES
NO
HOW MUCH DOES IT COST?
AVAILABLE NOW?
__ DAYS?
__ WEEKS?

. Heeft u 95 oktaan benzine?

. Super?

. Loodvrij?

. Is dit de hoofdweg naar __ ?

. Gaat deze weg naar __ ?

. Links af

. Rechtdoor

. Rechts af

. Achter

0. Is hier een motorfiets reparatiewerkplaats in de buurt?

1. Hoeveel kilometer ongeveer?

)NDERDELEN EN SERVICE

2. Ik heb een lege akku. Heeft u startkabels?

3. De plus (+) pool

4. De min (–) pool

5. Kunt u mijn akku opladen?

6. Kunt u mij alstublieft aanduwen?

7. Heeft u gedestilleerd water?

8. Heeft u een nieuwe akku?

9. Kunt u de klepspeling afstellen?
De inlaatklepspeling is __ , de uitlaatklepseling is __ .

0. Heeft u klepstelplaatjes?

1. De motor start niet. Kunt u de oorzaak opsporen?

2. De motor draait onregelmatig. Kunt u de oorzaak opsporen?

3. Ik hoor een abnormaal geluid uit de motor.
Kunt u de oorzaak opsporen?

JA
NEE
HOEVEEL KOST HET?
NU LEVERBAAR?
__ DAGEN?
__ WEKEN?

24. I have an unusual sound in the gear box.
Can you check-out the problem?

25. I have an unusual sound in the final drive.
Can you check-out the problem?

26. Can you service my cooling system?

27. Can you change the thermostat?

28. Can you tighten the spokes?

29. Can you service my front brakes?

30. Can you service my rear brakes?

31. Can you change the oil in my motorcycle?

32. Can you fix a puncture?

33. Do you have compressed air?

34. Do you have anti-freeze?

35. Do you have brake/clutch fluid?

36. Do you have 4-stroke engine oil?

37. Do you have 2-stroke engine oil?

38. Do you have octane booster?

39. I need a tubeless type front tire. Do you have a __ x __ x __ tire?

40. I need a tubeless type rear tire. Do you have a __ x __ x __ tire?

41. I need a tube type front tire. Do you have a __ x __ x __ tire?

42. Do you have an inner tube for this tire?

43. I need a tube type rear tire. Do you have a __ x __ x __ tire?

44. Can you change the tire?

45. I need some spark plugs. Do you have this type?

46. I need an air filter. Do you have this type?

47. I need a fuel filter. Do you have this type?

48. I need an oil filter. Do you have this type?

YES
NO
HOW MUCH DOES IT COST?
AVAILABLE NOW?
__ DAYS?
__ WEEKS?

24. Ik hoor een abnormaal geluid uit de versnellingsbak.
    Kunt u de oorzaak opsporen?

25. Ik hoor een abnormaal geluid uit de kardan. Kunt u er naar luisteren?

26. Kunt u een inspektie uitvoeren aan mijn koelsysteem?

27. Kunt u de thermostaat vervangen?

28. Kunt u de spaken naspannen?

29. Kunt u mijn voorrem inspekteren?

30. Kunt u mijn achterrem inspekteren?

31. Kunt u de olie van mijn motorfiets verversen?

32. Kunt u een lekke band repareren?

33. Heeft u perslucht?

34. Heeft u anti-vries (koelvloeistof)?

35. Heeft u rem/koppelings vloeistof?

36. Heeft u 4-takt motorolie?

37. Heeft u 2-takt motorolie?

38. Heeft u oktaan-booster?

39. Ik heb een tubeless voorband nodig. Heeft u een __ x __ x __ band?

40. Ik heb een tubeless achterband nodig. Heeft u een __ x __ x __ band?

41. Ik heb een voorband met binnenband nodig.
    Heeft u een __ x __ x __ band?

42. Heeft u een binnenband voor deze band?

43. Ik heb een achterband met binnenband nodig.
    Heeft u een __ x __ x __ band?

44. Kunt u de band verwisselen?

45. Ik heb bougies nodig. Heeft u dit type?

46. Ik heb een luchtfilter element nodig. Heeft u dit type?

47. Ik heb een benzinefilter nodig. Heeft u dit type?

48. Ik heb een oliefilter nodig. Heeft u dit type?

JA
NEE
HOEVEEL KOST HET?
NU LEVERBAAR?
__ DAGEN?
__ WEKEN?

49. Do you have a brake cable?

50. Do you have a choke cable?

51. Do you have a clutch cable?

52. Do you have a speedometer cable?

53. Do you have a throttle cable?

54. Do you have a 10 amp fuse?

55. Do you have a 15 amp fuse?

56. Do you have a main fuse?

57. Do you have starter brushes?

58. Do you have a bus or blade fuse?

59. Do you have an ACG plug?

60. Do you have a head light bulb/globe?

61. Do you have a tail light bulb/globe?

62. Do you have a turn indicator bulb/globe?

63. Do you have instrument bulbs/globes?

64. Do you have valve/rocker cover gaskets?

65. Do you have valve/rocker cover bolt packings?

66. Do you have a chain and sprocket?

67. Do you have a master link/drive chain joint?

FRAME & ENGINE WORDS

68. Alternator/generator

69. Battery

70. Bolt

71. Brake pad

72. Brake shoes

73. Carburetor

74. Chain

YES
NO
HOW MUCH DOES IT COST?
AVAILABLE NOW?
__ DAYS?
__ WEEKS?

272

DUTCH
(NEDERLANDS)

TRANSLATED BY HONDA OF THE NETHERLANDS

The
ENDLESS
RIDE

49. Heeft u een remkabel?

50. Heeft u een choke kabel?

51. Heeft u een koppelingskabel?

52. Heeft u een snelheidsmeterkabel?

53. Heeft u een gaskabel?

54. Heeft u een 10 ampère zekering?

55. Heeft u een 15 ampère zekering?

56. Heeft u een hoofd zekering?

57. Heeft u koolborstels voor de startmotor?

58. Heeft u een glas of een platte zekering?

59. Heeft u een ACG plug?

60. Heeft u een koplamp?

61. Heeft u een achterlampje?

62. Heeft u een lampje voor het knipperlicht?

63. Heeft u lampjes voor het instrumentenpaneel?

64. Heeft u een klepdeksel pakking?

65. Heeft u rubber afdichtingen voor de klepdeksel bouten?

66. Heeft u een ketting en tandwielen?

67. Heeft u een sluitschakel voor de ketting?

FRAME EN MOTOR

68. AC-generator, dynamo

69. Akku

70. Tapeind

71. Remblok

72. Remschoen

73. Karburateur

74. Ketting

JA
NEE
HOEVEEL KOST HET?
NU LEVERBAAR?
__ DAGEN?
__ WEKEN?

273

75. Clutch

76. Diodes

77. Drive flange

78. Drive line

79. Drive shaft

80. Electrical wire

81. Fuel pump

82. Gear box

83. Lock nut

84. Machine screw

85. Master link/drive chain joint

86. Nut

87. Rectifier

88. Rotor

89. Sheet metal screw

90. Solenoid

91. Starter motor

92. Valve

93. Washer

94. Wheel bearing

95. Wire

YES
NO
HOW MUCH DOES IT COST?
AVAILABLE NOW?
__ DAYS?
__ WEEKS?

DUTCH
(NEDERLANDS)

TRANSLATED BY HONDA OF THE NETHERLANDS

The
ENDLESS
RIDE

75. Koppeling

76. Diode

77. Aandrijfflens

78. Aandrijflijn

79. Aandrijfas (kardanas)

80. Elektriciteitsdraad

81. Benzinepomp

82. Versnellingsbak

83. Zelfborgende moer

84. Bout

85. Moer

86. Sluitschakel

87. Gelijkrichter

88. Rotor

89. Plaatschroef (Parker, zelftappende schroef)

90. Spoel

91. Startmotor

92. Klep

93. Sluitring

94. Wiellager

95. Draad

JA
NEE
HOEVEEL KOST HET?
NU LEVERBAAR?
__ DAGEN?
__ WEKEN?

AT THE REFUELING STATION

1. Do you have 95 octane, leaded or 4-Star?
2. Super?
3. Unleaded?
4. Is this the main road to __ ?
5. Will this road go to __ ?
6. To the left
7. Straight ahead
8. To the right
9. Behind
10. Is there a motorcycle repair shop near here?
11. About how many kilometers to __ ?

PARTS & SERVICE

12. I have a dead battery. Do you have jumper cables/jump leads?
13. The Positive (+) Terminal
14. The Negative (-) Terminal
15. Can you charge my battery?
16. Can you please give me a push start/bump start?
17. Do you have distilled water?
18. Do you have a new battery?
19. Can you adjust my valves? My intake is __ , my exhaust is __ .
20. Do you have shims?
21. The engine won't start. Can you check-out the problem?
22. The engine is running rough. Can you check-out the problem?
23. I have an unusual sound in the engine.
    Can you check-out the problem?

YES
NO
HOW MUCH DOES IT COST?
AVAILABLE NOW?
__ DAYS?
__ WEEKS?

FRENCH
(FRANCAIS)

TRANSLATED BY HONDA OF FRANCE

The
ENDLESS
RIDE

À LA STATION SERVICE

1. Avez-vous de l'octane 95?

2. Du super?

3. Du sans plomb?

4. Est-ce bien la route de __ ?

5. Est-ce que cette route va à __ ?

6. A gauche

7. Tout droit

8. A droite

9. A côté de

10. Y a t-il un réparateur de moto près d'ici?

11. A environ combien de kilomètres?

PIÈCES ET APRÉS-VENTE

12. Ma batterie est déchargée. Avez-vous des câbles?

13. Pôle positif (+)

14. Pôle négatif (-)

15. Pouvez-vous recharger ma batterie?

16. Pouvez-vous m'aider à pousser pour démarrer?

17. Avez-vous de l'eau déminéralisée?

18. Avez-vous une batterie neuve?

19. Pouvez-vous régler le jeu aux soupapes? Admission __ , Echappement __ .

20. Avez-vous les pastilles de réglage?

21. Le moteur ne démarrera pas. Pouvez-vous trouver l'origine de la panne?

22. Le moteur ne tourne pas rond. Pouvez-vous trouver l'origine de la panne?

23. Le moteur fait un bruit inhabituel.
Pouvez-vous trouver l'origine de la panne?

> *OUI*
> *NON*
> *COMBIEN CELA COÛTE T-IL?*
> *DISPONIBLE IMMÉDIATEMENT?*
> *__ DANS COMBIEN DE JOURS?*
> *__ DANS COMBIEN DE SEMAINES?*

24. I have an unusual sound in the gear box.
Can you check-out the problem?

25. I have an unusual sound in the final drive.
Can you check-out the problem?

26. Can you service my cooling system?

27. Can you change the thermostat?

28. Can you tighten the spokes?

29. Can you service my front brakes?

30. Can you service my rear brakes?

31. Can you change the oil in my motorcycle?

32. Can you fix a puncture?

33. Do you have compressed air?

34. Do you have anti-freeze?

35. Do you have brake/clutch fluid?

36. Do you have 4-stroke engine oil?

37. Do you have 2-stroke engine oil?

38. Do you have octane booster?

39. I need a tubeless type front tire.
Do you have a __ x __ x __ tire?

40. I need a tubeless type rear tire.
Do you have a __ x __ x __ tire?

41. I need a tube type front tire.
Do you have a __ x __ x __ tire?

42. Do you have an inner tube for this tire?

43. I need a tube type rear tire.
Do you have a __ x __ x __ tire?

44. Can you change the tire?

45. I need some spark plugs. Do you have this type?

46. I need an air filter. Do you have this type?

YES
NO
HOW MUCH DOES IT COST?
AVAILABLE NOW?
__ DAYS?
__ WEEKS?

4. La boîte de vitesse fait un bruit inhabituel.
   Pouvez-vous trouver l'origine de la panne?

5. La transmission fait un bruit inhabituel.
   Pouvez-vous trouver l'origine de la panne?

6. Pouvez-vous vidanger le système de refroidissement?

7. Pouvez-vous changer le thermostat?

8. Pouvez-vous retendre les rayons?

9. Pouvez-vous contrôler le frein avant?

0. Pouvez-vous contrôler le frein arrière?

1. Pouvez-vous changer l'huile de ma moto?

2. Pouvez-vous réparer une crevaison?

3. Avez-vous de l'air comprimé?

4. Avez-vous de l'anti-gel?

5. Avez-vous du liquide hydraulique pour frein/embrayage?

6. Avez-vous de l'huile pour moteur 4 temps?

7. Avez-vous de l'huile pour moteur 2 temps?

8. Avez-vous de l'additif élévateur d'octane?

9. J'ai besoin d'un pneu avant type tubeless.
   Avez-vous un pneu __ x __ x __ ?

0. J'ai besoin d'un pneu arrière type tubeless.
   Avez-vous un pneu __ x __ x __ ?

1. J'ai besoin d'un pneu avant avec chambre à air.
   Avez-vous un pneu __ x __ x __ pneu?

2. Avez-vous une chambre à air pour ce pneu?

3. J'ai besoin d'un pneu arrière avec chambre à air.
   Avez-vous un pneu __ x __ x __ ?

4. Pouvez-vous changer le pneu?

5. J'ai besoin de bougies. Avez-vous ce type?

6. J'ai besoin d'un filtre à air. Avez-vous ce type?

OUI
NON
COMBIEN CELA COÛTE T-IL?
DISPONIBLE IMMÉDIATEMENT?
__ DANS COMBIEN DE JOURS?
__ DANS COMBIEN DE SEMAINES?

47. I need a fuel filter. Do you have this type?

48. I need an oil filter. Do you have this type?

49. Do you have a brake cable?

50. Do you have a choke cable?

51. Do you have a clutch cable?

52. Do you have a speedometer cable?

53. Do you have a throttle cable?

54. Do you have a 10 amp fuse?

55. Do you have a 15 amp fuse?

56. Do you have a main fuse?

57. Do you have starter brushes?

58. Do you have a bus or blade fuse?

59. Do you have an ACG plug?

60. Do you have a head light bulb/globe?

61. Do you have a tail light bulb/globe?

62. Do you have a turn indicator bulb/globe?

63. Do you have instrument bulbs/globes?

64. Do you have valve/rocker cover gaskets?

65. Do you have valve/rocker cover bolt packings?

66. Do you have a chain and sprocket?

67. Do you have a master link/drive chain joint?

FRAME & ENGINE WORDS

68. Alternator/generator

69. Battery

70. Bolt

71. Brake pad

72. Brake shoes

YES
NO
HOW MUCH DOES IT COST?
AVAILABLE NOW?
__ DAYS?
__ WEEKS?

7. J'ai besoin d'un filtre à essence. Avez-vous ce type?

8. J'ai besoin d'un filtre à huile. Avez-vous ce type?

9. Avez-vous un câble de frein?

0. Avez-vous un câble de starter?

1. Avez-vous un câble d'embrayage?

2. Avez-vous un câble de compteur de vitesse?

3. Avez-vous un câble de gaz?

4. Avez-vous un fusible de 10 ampères?

5. Avez-vous un fusible de 15 ampères?

6. Avez-vous un fusible principal?

7. Avez-vous des charbons de démarreur? (démarreur électrique)

8. Avez-vous un fusible à lames?

9. Avez-vous une bougie d'allumage?

0. Avez-vous une ampoule de phare?

1. Avez-vous une ampoule de feu arrière?

2. Avez-vous une ampoule de clignotant?

3. Avez-vous une ampoule de tableau de bord?

4. Avez-vous des joints de couvercle de culasse?

5. Avez-vous une pochette de vis de couvercle de culasse?

6. Avez-vous une chaîne et une couronne?

7. Avez-vous une attache rapide?

ADRE ET MOTEUR : LEXIQUE

8. Alternateur/générateur

9. Batterie

0. Boulon

1. Plaquette de frein

2, Mâchoire de frein

> *OUI*
> *NON*
> *COMBIEN CELA COÛTE T-IL?*
> *DISPONIBLE IMMÉDIATEMENT?*
> *__ DANS COMBIEN DE JOURS?*
> *__ DANS COMBIEN DE SEMAINES?*

73. Carburetor

74. Chain

75. Clutch

76. Diodes

77. Drive flange

78. Drive line

79. Drive shaft

80. Electrical wire

81. Fuel pump

82. Gear box

83. Lock nut

84. Machine screw

85. Master link/drive chain joint

86. Nut

87. Rectifier

88. Rotor

89. Sheet metal screw

90. Solenoid

91. Starter motor

92. Valve

93. Washer

94. Wheel bearing

95. Wire

YES
NO
HOW MUCH DOES IT COST?
AVAILABLE NOW?
__ DAYS?
__ WEEKS?

3. Carburateur

4. Chaîne

5. Embrayage

6. Diodes

7. Flasque d'entraînement

8. Ligne d'arbre

9. Arbre moteur

0. Fil électrique

1. Pompe à essence

2. Boîte de vitesses

3. Contre écrou

4. Tournevis

5. Attache rapide

6. Ecrou

7. Redresseur

8. Rotor

9. Vis à tôle

0. Solenoïde

1. Démarreur

2. Soupape

3. Rondelle

4. Roulement de roue

5. Fil

OUI
NON
COMBIEN CELA COÛTE T-IL?
DISPONIBLE IMMÉDIATEMENT?
__ DANS COMBIEN DE JOURS?
__ DANS COMBIEN DE SEMAINES?

AT THE REFUELING STATION

1. Do you have 95 octane, leaded or 4-Star?
2. Super?
3. Unleaded?
4. Is this the main road to __ ?
5. Will this road go to __ ?
6. To the left
7. Straight ahead
8. To the right
9. Behind
10. Is there a motorcycle repair shop near here?
11. About how many kilometers to __ ?

PARTS & SERVICE

12. I have a dead battery. Do you have jumper cables/jump leads?
13. The Positive (+) Terminal
14. The Negative (-) Terminal
15. Can you charge my battery?
16. Can you please give me a push start/bump start?
17. Do you have distilled water?
18. Do you have a new battery?
19. Can you adjust my valves? My intake is __ , my exhaust is __ .
20. Do you have shims?
21. The engine won't start. Can you check-out the problem?
22. The engine is running rough. Can you check-out the problem?
23. I have an unusual sound in the engine.
    Can you check-out the problem?

YES
NO
HOW MUCH DOES IT COST?
AVAILABLE NOW?
__ DAYS?
__ WEEKS?

AN DER TANKSTELLE

1. Haben Sie 95 Oktan?
2. Super?
3. Bleifrei?
4. Ist dies die Hauptstraße nach __ ?
5. Führt diese Straße nach __ ?
6. Nach links
7. Geradeaus
8. Nach rechts
9. Hinter
10. Gibt es in der Nähe eine Motorradwerkstatt?
11. Wieviele km sind es?

ERSATZTEILE & KUNDENDIENST

12. Meine Batterie ist leer. Haben Sie Startkabel?
13. Der Pluspol (+)
14. Der Minuspol (-)
15. Können Sie meine Batterie laden?
16. Können Sie mich bitte anschieben?
17. Haben Sie destilliertes Wasser?
18. Haben sie eine neue Batterie?
19. Können Sie meine Ventile einstellen? Einlaß ist __ , der Auslaß ist __ .
20. Haben Sie Ventileinstellplättchen (Shims)?
21. Der Motor springt nicht an.
    Können Sie nachschauen, wo das Problem liegt?
22. Der Motor läuft rauh. Können Sie nachschauen, wo da Problem liegt?
23. Der Motor macht ein ungewohntes Geräusch.
    Können Sie nachschauen, wo das Problem liegt?

JA
NEIN
WIEVIEL KOSTET DAS?
HABEN SIE DAS VORRÄTIG?
__ TAGE?
__ WOCHEN?

285

24. I have an unusual sound in the gear box.
    Can you check-out the problem?

25. I have an unusual sound in the final drive.
    Can you check-out the problem?

26. Can you service my cooling system?

27. Can you change the thermostat?

28. Can you tighten the spokes?

29. Can you service my front brakes?

30. Can you service my rear brakes?

31. Can you change the oil in my motorcycle?

32. Can you fix a puncture?

33. Do you have compressed air?

34. Do you have anti-freeze?

35. Do you have brake/clutch fluid?

36. Do you have 4-stroke engine oil?

37. Do you have 2-stroke engine oil?

38. Do you have octane booster?

39. I need a tubeless type front tire.
    Do you have a __ x __ x __ tire?

40. I need a tubeless type rear tire.
    Do you have a __ x __ x __ tire?

41. I need a tube type front tire.
    Do you have a __ x __ x __ tire?

42. Do you have an inner tube for this tire?

43. I need a tube type rear tire.
    Do you have a __ x __ x __ tire?

44. Can you change the tire?

45. I need some spark plugs. Do you have this type?

46. I need an air filter. Do you have this type?

YES
NO
HOW MUCH DOES IT COST?
AVAILABLE NOW?
__ DAYS?
__ WEEKS?

24. Das Getriebe macht ein ungewohntes Geräusch. Können Sie nachschauen, wo das Problem liegt?

25. Der Endantrieb macht ein ungewöhnliches Geräusch. Können Sie nachschauen, wo das Problem liegt?

26. Können Sie mein Kühlsystem warten?

27. Können Sie das Thermostat wechseln?

28. Können Sie die Speichen festziehen?

29. Können Sie meine Vorderradbremse warten?

30. Können Sie meine Hinterradbremse warten?

31. Können Sie einen Ölwechsel machen?

32. Könne Sie einen Plattfuß flicken?

33. Haben Sie Druckluft?

34. Haben Sie Frostschutz?

35. Haben Sie Brems/Kupplungs-Flüssigkeit?

36. Haben Sie Viertakt-Öl?

37. Haben Sie Zweitakt-Öl?

38. Haben Sie Oktanadditiv?

39. Ich benötige einen schlauchlosen Vorderradreifen. Haben Sie einen __ x __ x __ Reifen?

40. Ich benötige einen schlauchlosen Hinterradreifen. Habe Sie einen __ x __ x __ Reifen?

41. Ich benötige einen Vorderradreifen mit Schlauch. Haben Sie einen __ x __ x __ Reifen?

42. Haben Sie einen Schlauch für diesen Reifen?

43. Ich benötige einen Hinterradreifen mit Schlauch. Haben Sie einen __ x __ x __ Reifen?

44. Können Sie diesen Reifen wechseln?

45. Ich benötige einige Zündkerzen. Haben Sie diesen Typ?

46. Ich benötige einen Luftfilter. Haben Sie diesen Typ?

JA
NEIN
WIEVIEL KOSTET DAS?
HABEN SIE DAS VORRÄTIG?
__ TAGE?
__ WOCHEN?

47. I need a fuel filter. Do you have this type?

48. I need an oil filter. Do you have this type?

49. Do you have a brake cable?

50. Do you have a choke cable?

51. Do you have a clutch cable?

52. Do you have a speedometer cable?

53. Do you have a throttle cable?

54. Do you have a 10 amp fuse?

55. Do you have a 15 amp fuse?

56. Do you have a main fuse?

57. Do you have starter brushes?

58. Do you have a bus or blade fuse?

59. Do you have an ACG plug?

60. Do you have a head light bulb/globe?

61. Do you have a tail light bulb/globe?

62. Do you have a turn indicator bulb/globe?

63. Do you have instrument bulbs/globes?

64. Do you have valve/rocker cover gaskets?

65. Do you have valve/rocker cover bolt packings?

66. Do you have a chain and sprocket?

67. Do you have a master link/drive chain joint?

FRAME & ENGINE WORDS

68. Alternator/generator

69. Battery

70. Bolt

71. Brake pad

72. Brake shoes

YES
NO
HOW MUCH DOES IT COST?
AVAILABLE NOW?
__ DAYS?
__ WEEKS?

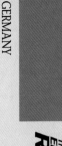

7. Ich benötige einen Benzinfilter. Haben Sie diesen Typ?

8. Ich benötige einen Ölfilter. Haben Sie diesen Typ?

9. Haben Sie einen Bremszug?

0. Haben Sie einen Chokezug?

1. Haben Sie einen Kupplungszug?

2. Haben Sie eine Tachowelle?

3. Haben Sie einen Gaszug?

4. Haben Sie eine Sicherung mit 10 Ampere?

5. Haben Sie eine Sicherung mit 15 Ampere?

6. Haben Sie eine Hauptsicherung?

7. Haben Sie Kohlebürsten für den Anlasser?

8. Haben Sie eine Hauptsicherung oder eine Stecksicherung?

9. Haben Sie ACG-Zündkerzen?

0. Haben Sie eine Birne für den Hauptscheinwerfer?

1. Haben Sie eine Birne für das Rücklicht?

2. Haben Sie eine Birne für den Blinker?

3. Haben Sie Birnen für die Instrumenten-Beleuchtung?

4. Haben Sie Ventildeckel-Dichtungen?

5. Haben Sie Dichtringe für die Ventildeckel-Schrauben?

6. Haben Sie eine Kette und Kettenrad?

7. Haben Sie ein Kettenschloß?

RAHMEN & MOTORBEGRIFFE

8. Drehstromlichtmaschine/Lichtmaschine

9. Batterie

0. Bolzen

1. Bremsbelag

2. Bremsbelag

JA
NEIN
WIEVIEL KOSTET DAS?
HABEN SIE DAS VORRÄTIG?
__ TAGE?
__ WOCHEN?

73. Carburetor
74. Chain
75. Clutch
76. Diodes
77. Drive flange
78. Drive line
79. Drive shaft
80. Electrical wire
81. Fuel pump
82. Gear box
83. Lock nut
84. Machine screw
85. Master link/drive chain joint
86. Nut
87. Rectifier
88. Rotor
89. Sheet metal screw
90. Solenoid
91. Starter motor
92. Valve
93. Washer
94. Wheel bearing
95. Wire

YES
NO
HOW MUCH DOES IT COST?
AVAILABLE NOW?
__ DAYS?
__ WEEKS?

GERMAN
(DEUTSCH)

TRANSLATED BY HONDA OF GERMANY

THE
ENDLESS
RIDE

73. Vergaser

74. Kette

75. Kupplung

76. Diode

77. Antriebsflansch

78. Antriebsstrang

79. Antriebswelle (Kardan)

80. Elektrokabel

81. Benzinpumpe

82. Getriebe

83. Sicherungsmutter

84. Maschinenschraube

85. Kettenglied

86. Nuss

87. Gleichrichter

88. Rotor

89. Blech-Schraube

90. Magnetschalter

91. Anlasser

92. Ventil

93. Unterlegscheibe, Ring

94. Radlager

95. Kabel

JA
NEIN
WIEVIEL KOSTET DAS?
HABEN SIE DAS VORRÄTIG?
__ TAGE?
__ WOCHEN?

AT THE REFUELING STATION

1. Do you have 95 octane, leaded or 4-Star?
2. Super?
3. Unleaded?
4. Is this the main road to __ ?
5. Will this road go to __ ?
6. To the left
7. Straight ahead
8. To the right
9. Behind
10. Is there a motorcycle repair shop near here?
11. About how many kilometers to __ ?

PARTS & SERVICE

12. I have a dead battery. Do you have jumper cables/jump leads?
13. The Positive (+) Terminal
14. The Negative (-) Terminal
15. Can you charge my battery?
16. Can you please give me a push start/bump start?
17. Do you have distilled water?
18. Do you have a new battery?
19. Can you adjust my valves? My intake is __ , my exhaust is __ .
20. Do you have shims?
21. The engine won't start. Can you check-out the problem?
22. The engine is running rough. Can you check-out the problem?

YES
NO
HOW MUCH DOES IT COST?
AVAILABLE NOW?
__ DAYS?
__ WEEKS?

ΣΤΟ ΒΕΝΖΙΝΑΔΙΚΟ

. Εχετε Βενζίνη με 95 οκτάνια ;

. ΣΟΥΠΕΡ ;

. ΑΜΟΛΥΒΔΗ ;

. Αυτός είναι ο δρόμος για __ ;

. Θα με πάει αυτός ο δρόμος στο __ ;

. Προς τα αριστερά

. Ευθεία

. Προς τα δεξιά

. Πίσω

0. Υπάρχει κάπου κοντά μας συνεργείο Μοτοσυκλετών ;

1. Περίπου πόσα χιλιόμετρα ;

ΝΤΑΛΛΑΚΙΚΑ & ΣΕΡΒΙΣ

2. Η μπαταρία μου είναι νεκρή, έχετε καλώδιο φορτίσεως ;

3. Το θετικό (+)

4. Το αρνητικό (–)

5. Μπορείτε να μου φορτήσετε την μπαταρία μου ;

6. Μπορείτε να σπρώξετε την μοτοσυκλέτα μου για να την ξεκινήσω ;

7. Εχετε αποσταγμένο νερό ;

8. Εχετε κανούργια μπαταρία ;

9. Μπορείτε να ρυθμίσετε τις βαλβίδες δες ; Η εισαγωγή είναι __ .
       Η εξαγωγή είναι __ .

20. Εχετε καπελώτα ή ρεγουλαδόρους ;

21. Ο κινητήρας μου δεν δουλεύει. Μπορείτε να κοιτάξετε ποιό είναι το
      πρόβλημα ;

22. Ο κινητήρας μου δουλεύει άγρια. Μπορείτε να κοιτάξετε ποιό είναι το
      πρόβλημα ;

NAI

OXI

ΠΟΣΟ ΧΟΣΤΟΖΕΙ;

ΔΙΑΘΕΕΣΙΜΟ ΤΩΡΑ ;

ΗΜΕΡΕΣ __ ;

ΕΒΔΟΜΑΔΕΣ __ ;

23. I have an unusual sound in the engine.
    Can you check-out the problem?

24. I have an unusual sound in the gear box.
    Can you check-out the problem?

25. I have an unusual sound in the final drive.
    Can you check-out the problem?

26. Can you service my cooling system?

27. Can you change the thermostat?

28. Can you tighten the spokes?

29. Can you service my front brakes?

30. Can you service my rear brakes?

31. Can you change the oil in my motorcycle?

32. Can you fix a puncture?

33. Do you have compressed air?

34. Do you have anti-freeze?

35. Do you have brake/clutch fluid?

36. Do you have 4-stroke engine oil?

37. Do you have 2-stroke engine oil?

38. Do you have octane booster?

39. I need a tubeless type front tire. Do you have a __ x __ x __ tire?

40. I need a tubeless type rear tire. Do you have a __ x __ x __ tire?

41. I need a tube type front tire. Do you have a __ x __ x __ tire?

42. Do you have an inner tube for this tire?

43. I need a tube type rear tire. Do you have a __ x __ x __ tire?

44. Can you change the tire?

45. I need some spark plugs. Do you have this type?

YES
NO
HOW MUCH DOES IT COST?
AVAILABLE NOW?
__ DAYS?
__ WEEKS?

GREEK
(ΕΛΛΗΝΙΚΆ)

TRANSLATED BY HONDA OF GREECE

The
ENDLESS
RIDE

23. Εχω έναν ασυνήθη θόρυβο στον κινητήρα. Μπορείτε να κοιτάξετε ποιό είναι το πρόβλημα ;

24. Εχω ένα ασύνηθες θόρυβο στο διαφορικό. Μπορείτε να κοιτάξετε ποιό είναι το πρόβλημα ;

25. Εχω ένα ασυνήθη θόρυβο στη τελική μετάδοση. Μπορείτε να κοιτάξετε ποιό είναι το πρόβλημα ;

26. Μπορείτε να τσεκάρετε το σύστημα ψύξεως του κινητήρα ;

27. Μπορείτε να αλλάξετε τον θερμοστάτη ;

28. Μπορείτε να σφίξετε τις βίδες ;

29. Μπορείτε να τσεκάρετε τα εμπρόσθια φρένα ;

30. Μπορείτε να τσεκάρετε τα οπίσθια φρένα ;

31. Μπορείτε να αλλάξετε τα λάδια της μοτοσυκλέτας ;

32. Μπορείτε να μου φτιάξετε το κλατάρισμα ;

33. Εχετε κομπρεσσέρ αέρος ;

34. Εχετε αντιψυκτικό ;

35. Εχετε υγρά φρένων ;

36. Εχετε λάδι για τετράχρονο κινητήρα ;

37. Εχετε λάδι για δίχρονο κινητήρο ;

38. Εχετε ενισχυτικό βενζίνης ;

39. Χρειάζομαι ελαστικό χωρίς σαμπρέλα. Εχετε ένα ___ x ___ x ___ ;

40. Χρειάζομαι ένα λάστιχο τύπου χωρίς σαμπρέλα. Εχετε ένα λάστιχο ___ x ___ x ___ ;

41 Χρειάζομαι ένα λάστιχο τύπου με σαμπρέλα. Εχετε ένα λάστιχο ___ x ___ x ___ ;

42. Εχετε σαμπρέλα για αυτό το λάστιχο ;

43. Χρειάζομαι ένα οπίσθιο λάστιχο τύπου χωρίς σαμπρέλα. Εχετε ένα ___ x ___ x ___ λάστιχο ;

44. Μπορείτε να μού αλλάξετε το λάστιχο ;

45. Χρειάζομαι μερικά μπουζί. Εχετε αυτόν τον τύπο ;

NAI
OXI
ΠΟΣΟ ΧΟΣΤΟΖΕΙ;
ΔΙΑΘΕΕΣΙΜΟ ΤΩΡΑ ;
ΗΜΕΡΕΣ ___ ;
ΕΒΔΟΜΑΔΕΣ ___ ;

46. I need an air filter. Do you have this type?

47. I need a fuel filter. Do you have this type?

48. I need an oil filter. Do you have this type?

49. Do you have a brake cable?

50. Do you have a choke cable?

51. Do you have a clutch cable?

52. Do you have a speedometer cable?

53. Do you have a throttle cable?

54. Do you have a 10 amp fuse?

55. Do you have a 15 amp fuse?

56. Do you have a main fuse?

57. Do you have starter brushes?

58. Do you have a bus or blade fuse?

59. Do you have an ACG plug?

60. Do you have a head light bulb/globe?

61. Do you have a tail light bulb/globe?

62. Do you have a turn indicator bulb/globe?

63. Do you have instrument bulbs/globes?

64. Do you have valve/rocker cover gaskets?

65. Do you have valve/rocker cover bolt packings?

66. Do you have a chain and sprocket?

67. Do you have a master link/drive chain joint?

FRAME & ENGINE WORDS

68. Alternator/generator

69. Battery

70. Bolt

71. Brake pad

YES
NO
HOW MUCH DOES IT COST?
AVAILABLE NOW?
__ DAYS?
__ WEEKS?

GREEK
(ΕΛΛΗΝΙΚΆ)

TRANSLATED BY HONDA OF GREECE

The
ENDLESS
RIDE

46. Χρειάζομαι ένα φίλτρο αέρος. Εχετε αυτόν τον τύπο ;

47. Χρειάζομαι φίλτρο βενζίνης. Εχετε αυτόν τον τύπο ;

48. Χρειάζομαι ένα φίλτρο λαδιού. Εχετε αυτόν τον τύπο ;

49. Εχετε συρματόσχοινο φρένου ;

50. Εχετε συρματόσχοινο αέρος ;

51. Εχετε συρματόσχοινο αμπραγιάζ ;

52. Εχετε συρματόσχοινο κοντέρ ;

53. Εχετε ντίζα γκαζιού ;

54. Εχετε ασφάλεια των 10 ΑΜΠΕΡ ;

55. Εχετε ασφάλεια των 15 ΑΜΠΕΡ ;

56. Εχετε την γενική ασφάλεια ;

57. Εχετε καρβουνάκια μίζας ;

58. Εχετε γυάλινη ή κεραμική ασφάλεια ;

59. Εχετε αντιπαρασιτικό μπουζί ;

60. Εχετε εμπρόσθιο φανάρι ;

61. Εχετε λάμπα ΣΤΟΠ ;

62. Εχετε λαμπάκι φλάς για τα όργανα ;

63. Εχετε λάμπες οργάνων (Καντράν) ;

64. Εχετε φλάντζες καπακιού βαλβίδων ;

65. Εχετε βίδες καπακιού κεφαλής ;

66. Εχετε αλυσίδα και γρανάζι ;

67. Εχετε ασφάλεια αλυσίδας ;

ΛΕΞΕΙΣ ΑΠΟ ΜΗΧΑΝΗ ΣΑΣΙ

68. Δυναμό/Γεννήτρια

69. Μπαταρία

70. Βίδα

71. Τακάκια

NAI

OXI

ΠΟΣΟ ΧΟΣΤΟΖΕΙ;

ΔΙΑΘΕΕΣΙΜΟ ΤΩΡΑ ;

ΗΜΕΡΕΣ ___ ;

ΕΒΔΟΜΑΔΕΣ ___ ;

297

72. Brake shoes
73. Carburetor
74. Chain
75. Clutch
76. Diodes
77. Drive flange
78. Drive line
79. Drive shaft
80. Electrical wire
81. Fuel pump
82. Gear box
83. Lock nut
84. Machine screw
85. Master link/drive chain joint
86. Nut
87. Rectifier
88. Rotor
89. Sheet metal screw
90. Solenoid
91. Starter motor
92. Valve
93. Washer
94. Wheel bearing
95. Wire

YES
NO
HOW MUCH DOES IT COST?
AVAILABLE NOW?
__ DAYS?
__ WEEKS?

72. Σιαγώνες
73. Καρμπυρατέρ
74. Αλυσίδα
75. Αμπραγιάζ
76. Διόδους
77. Κορώνα πηνίου
78. Αξονας διαφορικού
79. Αξονας διαφορικού
80. Ηλεκτρικά καλώδια
81. Τρόμπα Βενζίνης
82. Διαφορικό
83. Παξιμάδι ασφαλείας
84. Βίδα (με πάσο)
85. Ασφάλεια αλυσίδας
86. Παξιμάδι
87. Ανορθωτής
88. Ρότορας
89. Λαμαρινόβιδα
90. Σωληνοειδής
91. Μίζα
92. Βαλβίδα
93. Ροδέλα
94. Ρουλεμάν τροχού
95. Καλώδιο

NAI
OXI
ΠΟΣΟ ΧΟΣΤΟΖΕΙ;
ΔΙΑΘΕΕΣΙΜΟ ΤΩΡΑ ;
ΗΜΕΡΕΣ ___ ;
ΕΒΔΟΜΑΔΕΣ ___ ;

AT THE REFUELING STATION

1. Do you have 95 octane, leaded or 4-Star?

2. Super?

3. Unleaded?

4. Is this the main road to __ ?

5. Will this road go to __ ?

6. To the left

7. Straight ahead

8. To the right

9. Behind

10. Is there a motorcycle repair shop near here?

11. About how many kilometers to __ ?

PARTS & SERVICE

12. I have a dead battery. Do you have jumper cables/jump leads?

13. The Positive (+) Terminal

14. The Negative (-) Terminal

15. Can you charge my battery?

16. Can you please give me a push start/bump start?

17. Do you have distilled water?

18. Do you have a new battery?

19. Can you adjust my valves? My intake is __ , my exhaust is __ .

20. Do you have shims?

21. The engine won't start. Can you check-out the problem?

22. The engine is running rough. Can you check-out the problem?

23. I have an unusual sound in the engine.
Can you check-out the problem?

YES
NO
HOW MUCH DOES IT COST?
AVAILABLE NOW?
__ DAYS?
__ WEEKS?

ALLA STAZIONE DI SERVIZIO

1. Avete carburante con 95 ottani?

2. Super?

3. Senza piombo?

4. Questa è la strada principale per __ ?

5. Dove conduce questa strada __ ?

6. A sinistra

7. Diritto

8. A destra

9. Dalla parte opposta

10. Nelle vincinanze c'è un'officina per riparazione motocicli?

11. Quanti Km dista __ ?

ASSISTENZA E RICAMBI

12. Ho la batteria scarica. Avete dei cavi di collegamento?

13. Terminale positivo (+)

14. Terminale negativo (-)

15. Potete caricarmi la batteria?

16. Per favore, potete darmi una spinta?

17. Avete dell'acqua distillata?

18. Avete una batteria nuova?

19. Potete regolarmi il gioco valvole?
    Il gioco valvole di aspirazione è __ , Il gioco valvole di scarico è __ .

20. Avete gli spessori?

21. Il motore non si vuole avviare. Potete effettuare un controllo?

22. Il motore gira in modo irregolare. Potete effettuare un controllo?

23. Il motore ha una rumorosità irregolare. Potete effettuare un controllo?

SI
NO
QUANTO COSTA?
DISPONIBILE SUBITO?
__ GIORNI?
__ SETTIMANE?

24. I have an unusual sound in the gear box.
    Can you check-out the problem?

25. I have an unusual sound in the final drive.
    Can you check-out the problem?

26. Can you service my cooling system?

27. Can you change the thermostat?

28. Can you tighten the spokes?

29. Can you service my front brakes?

30. Can you service my rear brakes?

31. Can you change the oil in my motorcycle?

32. Can you fix a puncture?

33. Do you have compressed air?

34. Do you have anti-freeze?

35. Do you have brake/clutch fluid?

36. Do you have 4-stroke engine oil?

37. Do you have 2-stroke engine oil?

38. Do you have octane booster?

39. I need a tubeless type front tire.
    Do you have a __ x __ x __ tire?

40. I need a tubeless type rear tire.
    Do you have a __ x __ x __ tire?

41. I need a tube type front tire.
    Do you have a __ x __ x __ tire?

42. Do you have an inner tube for this tire?

43. I need a tube type rear tire.
    Do you have a __ x __ x __ tire?

44. Can you change the tire?

45. I need some spark plugs. Do you have this type?

46. I need an air filter. Do you have this type?

YES
NO
HOW MUCH DOES IT COST?
AVAILABLE NOW?
__ DAYS?
__ WEEKS?

4. C'è una rumorosità irregolare nella scatola del cambio. Potete effettuare un controllo?

5. C'è una rumorosità irregolare nella trasmissione finale. Potete effettuare un controllo?

6. Potete controllare il circuito di raffreddamento?

7. Potete sostituirmi il termostato?

8. Potete serrarmi i raggi?

9. Potete controllare il freno anteriore?

0. Potete controllare il freno posteriore?

1. Potete sostituire l'olio alla mia moto?

2. Potete ripararmi una foratura?

3. Avete un compressore d'aria?

4. Avete del liquido antigelo?

5. Avete del liquido freni/frizione?

6. Avete olio per motore a quattro tempi?

7. Avete olio per motore a due tempi?

8. Avete un additivo per aumentare il Numero di Ottani?

9. Ho necessità di un pneumatico anteriore tipo "tubeless." Avete un pneumatico tipo __ x __ x __ ?

0. Ho necessità di un pneumatico posteriore tipo "tubeless." Avete un pneumatico tipo __ x __ x __ ?

1. Ho necessità di un pneumatico anteriore con camera d'aria. Avete un pneumatico tipo __ x __ x __ ?

2. Avete una camera d'aria per questo pneumatico?

3. Avete necessità di un pneumatico posteriore con camera d'aria. Avete un pneumatico tipo __ x __ x __ ?

4. Potete sostituirmi il pneumatico?

5. Ho necessità di alcune candele di accensione. Ne avete di questo tipo?

6. Ho necessità di un filtro aria. Ne avete di questo tipo?

SI
NO
QUANTO COSTA?
DISPONIBILE SUBITO?
__ GIORNI?
__ SETTIMANE?

47. I need a fuel filter. Do you have this type?

48. I need an oil filter. Do you have this type?

49. Do you have a brake cable?

50. Do you have a choke cable?

51. Do you have a clutch cable?

52. Do you have a speedometer cable?

53. Do you have a throttle cable?

54. Do you have a 10 amp fuse?

55. Do you have a 15 amp fuse?

56. Do you have a main fuse?

57. Do you have starter brushes?

58. Do you have a bus or blade fuse?

59. Do you have an ACG plug?

60. Do you have a head light bulb/globe?

61. Do you have a tail light bulb/globe?

62. Do you have a turn indicator bulb/globe?

63. Do you have instrument bulbs/globes?

64. Do you have valve/rocker cover gaskets?

65. Do you have valve/rocker cover bolt packings?

66. Do you have a chain and sprocket?

67. Do you have a master link/drive chain joint?

FRAME & ENGINE WORDS

68. Alternator/generator

69. Battery

70. Bolt

71. Brake pad

72. Brake shoes

YES
NO
HOW MUCH DOES IT COST?
AVAILABLE NOW?
__ DAYS?
__ WEEKS?

ITALIAN
(ITALIANO)

TRANSLATED BY HONDA OF ITALY

The
ENDLESS
RIDE

7. Ho necessità di un filtro carburante. Ne avete di questo tipo?

8. Ho necessità di un filtro olio. Ne avete di questo tipo?

9. Avete un cavo freno?

0. Avete un cavo starter?

1. Avete un cavo frizione?

2. Avete un cavo tachimetro?

3. Avete un cavo farfalla carburatore?

4. Avete un fusibile da 10 Ampere?

5. Avete un fusibile da 15 Ampere?

6. Avete un fusibile principale?

7. Avete spazzole per il motorino di avviamento?

8. Avete un fusibile a bulbo o a lama?

9. Avete un cappuccio per candele (ACG)?

0. Avete una lampadina faro anteriore?

1. Avete una lampadina luce posteriore?

2. Avete una lampadina per gli indicatori di direzione?

3. Avete una lampadina per la strumentazione?

4. Avete una guarnizione coperchio punterie?

5. Avete del sigillante per il coperchio punterie?

6. Avete una catena di trasmissione finle ed un pignone?

7. Avete una maglia di giunzione?

VOCABOLI MOTORE E TELAIO

8. Alternatore/generatore

9. Batteria

0. Bullone

1. Pasticca freno

2. Ganascia freno

SI
NO
QUANTO COSTA?
DISPONIBILE SUBITO?
__ GIORNI?
__ SETTIMANE?

73. Carburetor
74. Chain
75. Clutch
76. Diodes
77. Drive flange
78. Drive line
79. Drive shaft
80. Electrical wire
81. Fuel pump
82. Gear box
83. Lock nut
84. Machine screw
85. Master link/drive chain joint
86. Nut
87. Rectifier
88. Rotor
89. Sheet metal screw
90. Solenoid
91. Starter motor
92. Valve
93. Washer
94. Wheel bearing
95. Wire

YES
NO
HOW MUCH DOES IT COST?
AVAILABLE NOW?
__ DAYS?
__ WEEKS?

ITALIAN
(ITALIANO)

TRANSLATED BY HONDA OF ITALY

The
ENDLESS
RIDE

3. Carburatore

4. Catena

5. Frizione

6. Diodi

7. Flangia ruota

8. Trasmissione

9. Albero di trasmissione

0. Cavo elettrico

1. Pompa carburante

2. Scatola cambio

3. Controdado

4. Vite a ferro

5. Maglia di giunzione

6. Dado

7. Raddrizzatore

8. Rotore

9. Vite per lamiera

0. Solenoide

1. Motorino di avviamento

2. Valvola

3. Rondella

4. Cuscinetto ruota

5. Cavo elettrico

SI
NO
QUANTO COSTA?
DISPONIBILE SUBITO?
__ GIORNI?
__ SETTIMANE?

AT THE REFUELING STATION

1. Do you have 95 octane, leaded or 4-Star?
2. Super?
3. Unleaded?
4. Is this the main road to __ ?
5. Will this road go to __ ?
6. To the left
7. Straight ahead
8. To the right
9. Behind
10. Is there a motorcycle repair shop near here?
11. About how many kilometers to __ ?

PARTS & SERVICE

12. I have a dead battery. Do you have jumper cables/jump leads?
13. The Positive (+) Terminal
14. The Negative (-) Terminal
15. Can you charge my battery?
16. Can you please give me a push start/bump start?
17. Do you have distilled water?
18. Do you have a new battery?
19. Can you adjust my valves? My intake is __ , my exhaust is __ .
20. Do you have shims?
21. The engine won't start. Can you check-out the problem?
22. The engine is running rough. Can you check-out the problem?
23. I have an unusual sound in the engine.
Can you check-out the problem?

YES
NO
HOW MUCH DOES IT COST?
AVAILABLE NOW?
__ DAYS?
__ WEEKS?

O POSTO DE GASOLINA

. Tem 95 octanas?

. Super?

. Sem chumbo?

. É este o melhor caminho para __ ?

. Esta rua vai para __ ?

. À esquerda

. Sempre em frente

. À direita

. De trás

0. Existe aqui perto uma oficina de motos?

1 Quantos km?

PEÇAS & SERVIÇO

2. Tenho a bateria descarregada. Tem cabos de ligação?

3. O terminal (+) positivo

4. O terminal (-) negativo

5. Pode carregar a minha bateria?

6. Pode dar-me um empurrão?

7. Tem água destilada?

8. Tem baterias novas?

9. Pode ajustar as válvulas? A admissão está __ , o escape está __ .

0. Tem pastilhas?

1. O motor não trabalha. Pode verificar qual é o problema?

2. O motor funciona mal. Pode verificar qual o problema?

3. O motor está a fazer um barulho anormal.
Pode Verificar qual é o problema?

SIM
NÃO
QUANTO CUSTA?
ESTÁ DISPONIVEL JÁ?
__ DIAS?
__ SEMANAS?

24. I have an unusual sound in the gear box.
Can you check-out the problem?

25. I have an unusual sound in the final drive.
Can you check-out the problem?

26. Can you service my cooling system?

27. Can you change the thermostat?

28. Can you tighten the spokes?

29. Can you service my front brakes?

30. Can you service my rear brakes?

31. Can you change the oil in my motorcycle?

32. Can you fix a puncture?

33. Do you have compressed air?

34. Do you have anti-freeze?

35. Do you have brake/clutch fluid?

36. Do you have 4-stroke engine oil?

37. Do you have 2-stroke engine oil?

38. Do you have octane booster?

39. I need a tubeless type front tire.
Do you have a __ x __ x __ tire?

40. I need a tubeless type rear tire.
Do you have a __ x __ x __ tire?

41. I need a tube type front tire.
Do you have a __ x __ x __ tire?

42. Do you have an inner tube for this tire?

43. I need a tube type rear tire. Do you have a __ x __ x __ tire?

44. Can you change the tire?

45. I need some spark plugs. Do you have this type?

46. I need an air filter. Do you have this type?

47. I need a fuel filter. Do you have this type?

YES
NO
HOW MUCH DOES IT COST?
AVAILABLE NOW?
__ DAYS?
__ WEEKS?

PORTUGUESE
(PORTUGUÊS)

TRANSLATED BY HONDA OF PORTUGAL

The
ENDLESS
RIDE

4. A caixa de velocidades está a fazer um barulho anormal.
   Pode verificar o problema?

5. A transmissão está a fazer um barulho anormal.
   Pode verificar qualé o problema?

6. Pode reparar o sistema de arrefecimento?

7. Pode trocar o termostato?

8. Pode ajustar o raio das rodas?

9. Pode verificar os travões da frente?

0. Pode verificar os raios dos travões?

1. Pode mudar o óleo da mota?

2. Pode arranjar um furo no pneu?

3. Tem ar comprimido?

4. Tem anti-congelante?

5. Tem fluído para embraiagem/travões?

6. Tem óleo para motor de quatro tempos?

7. Tem óleo para motor de dois tempos?

8. Tem aditivo para gasolina?

9. Necessito de um pneu dianteiro sem câmara de ar.
   Tamanho __ x __ x __ ?

0. Necessito de um pneu traseiro sem câmara de ar.
   Tamanho __ x __ x __ ?

1. Necessito de um pneu com câmara de ar. Tamanho __ x __ x __ ?

2. Tem uma câmara de ar para este pneu?

3. Necessito de uma roda traseira com tubo Interior.
   Tem o Tamanho __ x __ x __ ?

4. Pode mudar este pneu?

5. Necessito de algumas velas. Tem deste tipo?

6. Necessito de um filtro de ar. Tem deste tipo?

7. Necessito de um filtro de combustivel. Tem deste tipo?

SIM
NÃO
QUANTO CUSTA?
ESTÁ DISPONIVEL JÁ?
__ DIAS?
__ SEMANAS?

48. I need an oil filter. Do you have this type?

49. Do you have a brake cable?

50. Do you have a choke cable?

51. Do you have a clutch cable?

52. Do you have a speedometer cable?

53. Do you have a throttle cable?

54. Do you have a 10 amp fuse?

55. Do you have a 15 amp fuse?

56. Do you have a main fuse?

57. Do you have starter brushes?

58. Do you have a bus or blade fuse?

59. Do you have an ACG plug?

60. Do you have a head light bulb/globe?

61. Do you have a tail light bulb/globe?

62. Do you have a turn indicator bulb/globe?

63. Do you have instrument bulbs/globes?

64. Do you have valve/rocker cover gaskets?

65. Do you have valve/rocker cover bolt packings?

66. Do you have a chain and sprocket?

67. Do you have a master link/drive chain joint?

FRAME & ENGINE WORDS

68. Alternator/generator

69. Battery

70. Bolt

71. Brake pad

72. Brake shoes

73. Carburetor

YES
NO
HOW MUCH DOES IT COST?
AVAILABLE NOW?
__ DAYS?
__ WEEKS?

PORTUGUESE
(PORTUGUÊS)

TRANSLATED BY HONDA OF PORTUGAL

The
ENDLESS
RIDE

8. Necessito de um filtro de óleo. Tem deste tipo?

9. Tem um cabo de travão?

0. Tem um cabo regulador de ar?

1. Tem um cabo de embraiagem?

2. Tem um cabo de velocimetro?

3. Tem um cabo de acelarador?

4. Tem um fusivel de 10 amperes?

5. Tem um fusivel de 15 amperes?

6. Tem um fusivel principal?

7. Tem escovas de motor de arranque?

8. Tem um fusivel comum?

9. Tem uma ficha para alternador?

0. Tem farois dianteiros?

1. Tem uma lâmpada traseira?

2. Tem uma lâmpada indicadora de mudança de direcção?

3. Tem lâmpadas para o painel de instrumentos?

4. Tem uma junta para a tampa das válvulas?

5. Tem casquilhos para parafusos do tampo das válvulas?

6. Tem carretos e correntes de transmissão?

7. Tem um elo principal?

PALAVRAS PARA QUADRO E MOTOR

8. Alternador/gerador

9. Bateria

0. Parafuso

1. Pastilhas do travão

2. Calço de travão

3. Carburador

SIM
NÃO
QUANTO CUSTA?
ESTÁ DISPONIVEL JÁ?
__ DIAS?
__ SEMANAS?

74. Chain
75. Clutch
76. Diodes
77. Drive flange
78. Drive line
79. Drive shaft
80. Electrical wire
81. Fuel pump
82. Gear box
83. Lock nut
84. Machine screw
85. Master link/drive chain joint
86. Nut
87. Rectifier
88. Rotor
89. Sheet metal screw
90. Solenoid
91. Starter motor
92. Valve
93. Washer
94. Wheel bearing
95. Wire

YES
NO
HOW MUCH DOES IT COST?
AVAILABLE NOW?
__ DAYS?
__ WEEKS?

74. Corrente
75. Embraiagem
76. Díodos
77. Falange condutora
78. Linha condutora
79. Veio de transmissão
80. Fio eléctrico
81. Bomba de gasolina
82. Caixa de velocidade
83. Porca de segurança/contraporca
84. Parafuso de rosca fina
85. Elo principal
86. Porca
87. Rectificador de corrente
88. Rotor
89. Parafuso para chapas
90. Solenoide
91. Motor de arranque
92. Válvula
93. Anilha
94. Rolamento de rodas
95. Fio

SIM
NÃO
QUANTO CUSTA?
ESTÁ DISPONIVEL JÁ?
__ DIAS?
__ SEMANAS?

AT THE REFUELING STATION

1. Do you have 95 octane, leaded or 4-Star?
2. Super?
3. Unleaded?
4. Is this the main road to __ ?
5. Will this road go to __ ?
6. To the left
7. Straight ahead
8. To the right
9. Behind
10. Is there a motorcycle repair shop near here?
11. About how many kilometers to __ ?

PARTS & SERVICE

12. I have a dead battery. Do you have jumper cables/jump leads?
13. The Positive (+) Terminal
14. The Negative (-) Terminal
15. Can you charge my battery?
16. Can you please give me a push start/bump start?
17. Do you have distilled water?
18. Do you have a new battery?
19. Can you adjust my valves? My intake is __ , my exhaust is __ .
20. Do you have shims?
21. The engine won't start. Can you check-out the problem?
22. The engine is running rough. Can you check-out the problem?
23. I have an unusual sound in the engine. Can you check-out the problem?

YES
NO
HOW MUCH DOES IT COST?
AVAILABLE NOW?
__ DAYS?
__ WEEKS?

EN LA ESTACIÓN DE GASOLINA

1. ¿Tiene 95 octano?

2. ¿Super?

3. ¿Sin Plomo?

4. ¿Es esté el camino principal a __ ?

5. ¿Irá este camino a __ ?

6. A la izquierda

7. Derecho

8. A la derecha

9. Atrás

10. ¿Habrá un taller de reparación de motocicleta cerca de aquí?

11. ¿Sobre cuántos kilometros?

REPUESTOS Y SERVICIO DE REPARACIÓN

12. Tengo una batería descargada. ¿Tiene cables de arranque/corriente?

13. El Terminal (+) Positivo

14. El Terminal (–) Negativo

15. ¿Puede cargarme la batería?

16. ¿Puede empujarme?

17. ¿Tiene agua distilada?

18. ¿Tiene una batería nueva?

19. ¿Puede ajustar las válvulas? Mi consumo es __ , y mi escape es __ .

20. ¿Tiene el eje oscilante/calzas?

21. El motor no arranca. ¿Puede inspeccionar el problema?

22. El motor esta corriendo agitado. ¿Puede inspeccionar el problema?

23. Hay un sonido raro en el motor. ¿Puede inspeccionar el problema?

SÍ
NO
¿CUANTO ES?
¿DISPONIBLE AHORA?
¿ __ DÍAS?
¿ __ SEMANAS?

24. I have an unusual sound in the gear box.
Can you check-out the problem?

25. I have an unusual sound in the final drive.
Can you check-out the problem?

26. Can you service my cooling system?

27. Can you change the thermostat?

28. Can you tighten the spokes?

29. Can you service my front brakes?

30. Can you service my rear brakes?

31. Can you change the oil in my motorcycle?

32. Can you fix a puncture?

33. Do you have compressed air?

34. Do you have anti-freeze?

35. Do you have brake/clutch fluid?

36. Do you have 4-stroke engine oil?

37. Do you have 2-stroke engine oil?

38. Do you have octane booster?

39. I need a tubeless type front tire.
Do you have a __ x __ x __ tire?

40. I need a tubeless type rear tire.
Do you have a __ x __ x __ tire?

41. I need a tube type front tire.
Do you have a __ x __ x __ tire?

42. Do you have an inner tube for this tire?

43. I need a tube type rear tire.
Do you have a __ x __ x __ tire?

44. Can you change the tire?

45. I need some spark plugs. Do you have this type?

46. I need an air filter. Do you have this type?

YES
NO
HOW MUCH DOES IT COST?
AVAILABLE NOW?
__ DAYS?
__ WEEKS?

SPANISH
(ESPAÑOL)

TRANSLATED BY HONDA OF SPAIN

The
ENDLESS
RIDE

4. Hay un sonido raro en la caja de cambio.
¿Puede inspeccionar el problema?

5. Hay un sonido raro en la transmisión.
¿Puede inspeccionar el problema?

6. ¿Puede cambiarme el agua del radiador?

7. ¿Puede cambiarme el termóstato?

8. ¿Puede ajustar los rayos de las llantas?

9. ¿Puede reparar los frenos delanteros?

0. ¿Puede reparar los frenos traseros?

1. ¿Puede cambiar el aceite en mi motocicleta?

2. ¿Puede arreglar el pinchazo en la neumático/llanta?

3. ¿Tiene aire a presión?

4. ¿Tiene anti-congelante?

5. ¿Tiene liquido de freno/embrague?

6. ¿Tiene aceite de motor cuatro tiempos?

7. ¿Tiene aceite de motor dos tiempos?

8. ¿Tiene aditivos para aumentare el poder de la gasolina/octano?

9. Necesito una llanta delantera sin cámara/tubo interior.
¿Tiene tamaño a __ x __ x __ de neumático/llanta?

0. Necesito una llanta trasera sin cámara/tubo interior.
¿Tiene tamaño a __ x __ x __ de neumático/llanta?

1. Necesito una llanta delantera con cámara/tubo interior.
¿Tiene tamaño a __ x __ x __ neumático/llanta?

2. ¿Tiene una cámara/tubo para esta neumático/llanta?

3. Necesito una llanta trasera con cámara interior.
¿Tiene tamaño a __ x __ x __ de neumático/llanta?

4. ¿Puede cambiar el neumático/la llanta?

5. Necesito unas bujías. ¿Tiene este tipo?

6 Necesito un filtro de aire. ¿Tiene de este tipo?

SÍ
NO
¿CUANTO ES?
¿DISPONIBLE AHORA?
¿ __ DÍAS?
¿ __ SEMANAS?

47. I need a fuel filter. Do you have this type?
48. I need an oil filter. Do you have this type?
49. Do you have a brake cable?
50. Do you have a choke cable?
51. Do you have a clutch cable?
52. Do you have a speedometer cable?
53. Do you have a throttle cable?
54. Do you have a 10 amp fuse?
55. Do you have a 15 amp fuse?
56. Do you have a main fuse?
57. Do you have starter brushes?
58. Do you have a bus or blade fuse?
59. Do you have an ACG plug?
60. Do you have a head light bulb/globe?
61. Do you have a tail light bulb/globe?
62. Do you have a turn indicator bulb/globe?
63. Do you have instrument bulbs/globes?
64. Do you have valve/rocker cover gaskets?
65. Do you have valve/rocker cover bolt packings?
66. Do you have a chain and sprocket?
67. Do you have a master link/drive chain joint?

FRAME & ENGINE WORDS

68. Alternator/generator
69. Battery
70. Bolt
71. Brake pad
72. Brake shoes

YES
NO
HOW MUCH DOES IT COST?
AVAILABLE NOW?
__ DAYS?
__ WEEKS?

SPANISH
(ESPAÑOL)

TRANSLATED BY HONDA OF SPAIN

The
ENDLESS
RIDE

47. Necesito un filtro de combustible. ¿Tiene uno de este tipo?

48. Necesito un filtro de aceite. ¿Tiene uno de este tipo?

49. ¿Tiene un cable de frenos?

50. ¿Tiene un cable regulador de aire?

51. ¿Tiene un cable de embrague?

52. ¿Tiene un cable de velocímetro?

53. ¿Tiene un cable de acelerador/regulador?

54. ¿Tiene un fusible de 10 amp (ampere)?

55. ¿Tiene un fusible de 15 amp (ampere)?

56. ¿Tiene un fusible principal?

57. ¿Tiene escobillas de arranque?

58. ¿Tiene un fusible de barra común o uno de álabe?

59. ¿Tiene una bujía de ACG?

60. ¿Tiene faro/foco delantero?

61. ¿Tiene una bombilla/foco piloto?

62. ¿Tiene una bombilla/foco para el intermitente?

63. ¿Tiene bombillas/focos para el tablero?

64. ¿Tiene retenes/empaques con válvulas forradas/tapaderas?

65. ¿Tiene retenes/empaques de pernos con válvulas forradas/tapaderas?

66. ¿Tiene una cadena y piñon/engrane?

67. ¿Tiene el eslabón principal?

BASTIDOR & MOTOR PALABRAS

68. Alternador/generador

69. Batería

70. Tornillo

71. Pastilla de freno

72. Zapata de freno

SÍ
NO
¿CUANTO ES?
¿DISPONIBLE AHORA?
¿ __ DÍAS?
¿ __ SEMANAS?

The ENDLESS RIDE

73. Carburetor

74. Chain

75. Clutch

76. Diodes

77. Drive flange

78. Drive line

79. Drive shaft

80. Electrical wire

81. Fuel pump

82. Gear box

83. Lock nut

84. Machine screw

85. Master link/drive chain joint

86. Nut

87. Rectifier

88. Rotor

89. Sheet metal screw

90. Solenoid

91. Starter motor

92. Valve

93. Washer

94. Wheel bearing

95. Wire

YES
NO
HOW MUCH DOES IT COST?
AVAILABLE NOW?
__ DAYS?
__ WEEKS?

SPANISH
(ESPAÑOL)

TRANSLATED BY HONDA OF SPAIN

The
ENDLESS
RIDE

3. Carburador
4. Cadena
5. Embrague
6. Diodos
7. Pestaña impulsor
8. —
9. Eje transmisor
0. Cableado/cable eléctrico
31. Bomba de gasolina
2. Caja de cambio
33. Contratuerca
34. Tornillo para metales
35. Eslabón principal
36. Tornillo
37. Rectificador de corriente
38. Rotor
39. Tornillo pasa fondos
0. Solenoide
1. Motor de arranque
2. Válvula
3. Arandela
4. Cojinete de rueda/llanta. Valero de rueda/llanta
5. Cableado/cable

SÍ
NO
¿CUANTO ES?
¿DISPONIBLE AHORA?
¿ __ DÍAS?
¿ __ SEMANAS?

AT THE REFUELING STATION

1. Do you have 95 octane, leaded or 4-Star?
2. Super?
3. Unleaded?
4. Is this the main road to __ ?
5. Will this road go to __ ?
6. To the left
7. Straight ahead
8. To the right
9. Behind
10. Is there a motorcycle repair shop near here?
11. About how many kilometers to __ ?

PARTS & SERVICE

12. I have a dead battery. Do you have jumper cables/jump leads?
13. The Positive (+) Terminal
14. The Negative (-) Terminal
15. Can you charge my battery?
16. Can you please give me a push start/bump start?
17. Do you have distilled water?
18. Do you have a new battery?
19. Can you adjust my valves? My intake is __ , my exhaust is __ .
20. Do you have shims?
21. The engine won't start. Can you check-out the problem?
22. The engine is running rough. Can you check-out the problem?
23. I have an unusual sound in the engine.
    Can you check-out the problem?

YES
NO
HOW MUCH DOES IT COST?
AVAILABLE NOW?
__ DAYS?
__ WEEKS?

. Har De 92 oktan?

. Super?

. Blyfri?

. Er dette hovedvejen til __ ?

. Fører denne vej til __ ?

. Til venstre

. Ligeud

. Til højre

. Bag/bagved

0. Er der et mc værksted i nærheden?

1. Cirka hvor mange kilometer?

RESERVEDELE & SERVICE

2. Mit batteri er dødt. Har De et startkabel?

3. Den positive (+) pol

4. Den negative (-) pol

5. Kan De oplade mit batteri?

6. Vil De være venlig at skubbe mig i gang?

7. Har De destilleret vand?

8. Har De et nyt batteri?

9. Kan De justere ventilerne?
Min indsugning er __ , min udstødning er __ .

0. Har De juster shims?

1. Motoren starter ikke. Kan De finde fejlen?

2. Motoren kører ujævnt. Kan De finde fejlen?

3. Der er en forkert lyd i motoren. Kan De finde fejlen?

JA
NEJ
HVAD KOSTER DET?
TILGÆNGELIG NU?
__ DAGE?
__ UGER?

325

24. I have an unusual sound in the gear box. Can you check-out the problem?

25. I have an unusual sound in the final drive. Can you check-out the problem?

26. Can you service my cooling system?

27. Can you change the thermostat?

28. Can you tighten the spokes?

29. Can you service my front brakes?

30. Can you service my rear brakes?

31. Can you change the oil in my motorcycle?

32. Can you fix a puncture?

33. Do you have compressed air?

34. Do you have anti-freeze?

35. Do you have brake/clutch fluid?

36. Do you have 4-stroke engine oil?

37. Do you have 2-stroke engine oil?

38. Do you have octane booster?

39. I need a tubeless type front tire. Do you have a __ x __ x __ tire?

40. I need a tubeless type rear tire. Do you have a __ x __ x __ tire?

41. I need a tube type front tire. Do you have a __ x __ x __ tire?

42. Do you have an inner tube for this tire?

43. I need a tube type rear tire. Do you have a __ x __ x __ tire?

44. Can you change the tire?

45. I need some spark plugs. Do you have this type?

46. I need an air filter. Do you have this type?

47. I need a fuel filter. Do you have this type?

48. I need an oil filter. Do you have this type?

49. Do you have a brake cable?

YES
NO
HOW MUCH DOES IT COST?
AVAILABLE NOW?
__ DAYS?
__ WEEKS?

DANISH
(DANSK)

TRANSLATED BY HONDA OF DENMARK

The
ENDLESS
RIDE

4. Gearkassen lyder forkert. Kan De finde fejlen?

5. Der er en forkert lyd i bagtøjet/kæden. Kan De finde fejlen?

6. Kan De ordne mit kølesystem?

7. Kan De udskifte termostaten?

8. Kan De spænde egerne?

9. Kan De checke mine forbremser?

0. Kan De ordne mine bagbremser?

1. Kan De skifte olie på min MC?

2. Kan De lappe mit dæk?

3. Har De trykluft?

4. Har De antifrostvæske?

5. Har De bremse/koblingsvæske?

6. Har De 4-takts motorolie?

7. Har De 2-takts motorolie?

8. Har De oktan forstærker?

9. Jeg mangler et slangeløst fordæk. Har De et __ x __ x __ dæk?

0. Jeg mangler et slangeløst bagdæk. Har De et __ x __ x __ dæk?

1. Jeg mangler et fordæk til slange.
Har De et __ x __ x __ dæk?

2. Har De en slange til det her hjul?

3. Jeg mangler et bagdæk til slange.
Har De et __ x __ x __ dæk?

4. Kan De skifte hjulet?

5. Jeg mangler tændrør. Har De denne type?

6. Jeg mangler et luftfilter. Har De denne type?

7. Jeg mangler et benzinfilter. Har De denne type?

8. Jeg mangler et oliefilter. Har De denne type?

9. Har De et bremsekabel?

_JA_
NEJ
HVAD KOSTER DET?
TILGÆNGELIG NU?
___ DAGE?_
___ UGER?_

327

50. Do you have a choke cable?

51. Do you have a clutch cable?

52. Do you have a speedometer cable?

53. Do you have a throttle cable?

54. Do you have a 10 amp fuse?

55. Do you have a 15 amp fuse?

56. Do you have a main fuse?

57. Do you have starter brushes?

58. Do you have a bus or blade fuse?

59. Do you have an ACG plug?

60. Do you have a head light bulb/globe?

61. Do you have a tail light bulb/globe?

62. Do you have a turn indicator bulb/globe?

63. Do you have instrument bulbs/globes?

64. Do you have valve/rocker cover gaskets?

65. Do you have valve/rocker cover bolt packings?

66. Do you have a chain and sprocket?

67. Do you have a master link/drive chain joint?

FRAME & ENGINE WORDS

68. Alternator/generator

69. Battery

70. Bolt

71. Brake pad

72. Brake shoes

73. Carburetor

74. Chain

75. Clutch

YES
NO
HOW MUCH DOES IT COST?
AVAILABLE NOW?
__ DAYS?
__ WEEKS?

DANISH
(DANSK)

TRANSLATED BY HONDA OF DENMARK

The
ENDLESS
RIDE

0. Har De et chokerkabel?

1. Har De et koblingskabel?

2. Har De et speedometerkabel?

3. Har De et gaskabel?

4. Har De en 10 ampere sikring?

5. Har De en 15 ampere sikring?

6. Har De en hovedsikring?

7. Har De starterkul?

8. Har De en glassikring eller en bladsikring?

9. Har De et ACG multistik?

0. Har De en forlygtepære?

1. Har De en pære til baglygten?

2. Har De en pære til blinklygten?

3. Har De pærer til instrumentbelysning?

4. Har De pakninger til ventildæksel?

5. Har De pakninger til ventildækselbolte?

6. Har De en kæde og kædehjul?

7. Har De et samleled?

TEL OG MOTOR ORD

8. Vekselstrømsgenerator

9. Batteri

0. Bolt

1. Bremseklods

2. Bremsesko

3. Karburator

4. Kæde

5. Kobling

JA
NEJ
HVAD KOSTER DET?
TILGÆNGELIG NU?
__ DAGE?
__ UGER?

329

76. Diodes
77. Drive flange
78. Drive line
79. Drive shaft
80. Electrical wire
81. Fuel pump
82. Gear box
83. Lock nut
84. Machine screw
85. Master link/drive chain joint
86. Nut
87. Rectifier
88. Rotor
89. Sheet metal screw
90. Solenoid
91. Starter motor
92. Valve
93. Washer
94. Wheel bearing
95. Wire

YES
NO
HOW MUCH DOES IT COST?
AVAILABLE NOW?
__ DAYS?
__ WEEKS?

6. Dioder

7. Kronhjul

8. Kraftoverføring

9. Kardanaksel

0. Elektrisk ledning

1. Benzinpumpe

2. Gearkasse

3. Låsemøtrik

4. Maskinskrue

5. Hoved forbindelse

6. Møtrik

7. Ensretter

8. Rotor

9. Selvskærende skrue

0. Relæ

1. Startmotor

2. Ventil

3. Spændeskive

4. Hjulleje

5. Lednin

JA
NEJ
HVAD KOSTER DET?
TILGÆNGELIG NU?
__ DAGE?
__ UGER?

331

AT THE REFUELING STATION

1. Do you have 95 octane, leaded or 4-Star?
2. Super?
3. Unleaded?
4. Is this the main road to __ ?
5. Will this road go to __ ?
6. To the left
7. Straight ahead
8. To the right
9. Behind
10. Is there a motorcycle repair shop near here?
11. About how many kilometers to __ ?

PARTS & SERVICE

12. I have a dead battery. Do you have jumper cables/jump leads?
13. The Positive (+) Terminal
14. The Negative (-) Terminal
15. Can you charge my battery?
16. Can you please give me a push start/bump start?
17. Do you have distilled water?
18. Do you have a new battery?
19. Can you adjust my valves? My intake is __ , my exhaust is __ .
20. Do you have shims?
21. The engine won't start. Can you check-out the problem?
22. The engine is running rough. Can you check-out the problem?
23. I have an unusual sound in the engine.
    Can you check-out the problem?

YES
NO
HOW MUCH DOES IT COST?
AVAILABLE NOW?
__ DAYS?
__ WEEKS?

POLTTOAINEEN JAKELUASEMALLA

. Onko Teillä 95 oktaania?

.. Korkeaoktaanista (Super)?

.. Lyijytöntä?

:. Onko tämä päätie __ ?

.. Viekö tämä tie __ ?

;. Vasemmalle

'. Suoraan eteenpäin

;. Oikealle

'. Takaisin/Taakse

0. Onko lähettyvillä moottoripyöräkorjaamoa?

1. Monenko km päässä __ ?

VARAOSAT & HUOLTO

2. Minulla on akku tyhjä. Onko Teillä apukäynnistyskaapeleita?

3. Plus (+) napa

4. Miinus (-) napa

5. Voisitteko ladata akkuni?

6. Voisitteko ystävällisesti auttaa työntämään pyöräni käyntiin?

7. Onko Teillä tislattua vettä?

8. Onko Teillä uutta akkua?

9. Voisitteko säätää venttiilit.
Imuventtiilin väljyys on __ , pakoventtiilin väljyys on __ .

20. Onko Teillä säätöpalat?

21. Moottori ei käynnisty. Voisitteko selvittää vian?

22. Moottori käy epätasaisesti. Voisitteko selvittää vian?

23. Moottorissa on epänormaali ääni. Voisitteko selvittää vian?

KYLLÄ
EI
PALJONKO MAKSAA?
SAATAVILLA NYT HETI?
__ PÄIVIEN KULUTTUA?
__ VIIKKOJEN KULUTTUA?

24. I have an unusual sound in the gear box.
Can you check-out the problem?

25. I have an unusual sound in the final drive.
Can you check-out the problem?

26. Can you service my cooling system?

27. Can you change the thermostat?

28. Can you tighten the spokes?

29. Can you service my front brakes?

30. Can you service my rear brakes?

31. Can you change the oil in my motorcycle?

32. Can you fix a puncture?

33. Do you have compressed air?

34. Do you have anti-freeze?

35. Do you have brake/clutch fluid?

36. Do you have 4-stroke engine oil?

37. Do you have 2-stroke engine oil?

38. Do you have octane booster?

39. I need a tubeless type front tire.
Do you have a __ x __ x __ tire?

40. I need a tubeless type rear tire.
Do you have a __ x __ x __ tire?

41. I need a tube type front tire.
Do you have a __ x __ x __ tire?

42. Do you have an inner tube for this tire?

43. I need a tube type rear tire. Do you have a __ x __ x __ tire?

44. Can you change the tire?

45. I need some spark plugs. Do you have this type?

46. I need an air filter. Do you have this type?

47. I need a fuel filter. Do you have this type?

YES
NO
HOW MUCH DOES IT COST?
AVAILABLE NOW?
__ DAYS?
__ WEEKS?

FINNISH
(SUOMEKSI)

TRANSLATED BY HONDA OF FINLAND

The
ENDLESS
RIDE

4. Vaihdelaatikossa on epänormaali ääni. Voisitteko selvittää vian?

5. Vetopyörästön kulmavaihteessa on epänormaali ääni. Voisitteko selvittaa vian?

6. Voisitteko huoltaa jäähdytysjärjestelmän?

7. Voisitteko vaihtaa termostaatin?

8. Voisitteko kiristää pyörien pinnat?

9. Voisitteko huoltaa etujarrut?

0. Voisitteko huoltaa takajarrut?

1. Voisitteko vaihtaa moottoriöljyt?

2. Voisitteko paikata renkaan?

3. Onko Teillä paineilmaa?

4. Onko Teillä jäähdytysnestettä?

5. Onko Teillä jarru/kytkinnestettä?

6. Onko Teillä 4-tahti moottoriöljyä?

7. Onko Teillä 2-tahti moottoriöljyä?

8. Onko Teillä ainetta, joka nostaa polttoaineen oktaanilukua?

9. Tarvitsen sisärenkaattoman eturenkaan.
Onko Teillä __ x __ x __ kokoista rengasta?

0. Tarvisen sisärenkaattoman takarenkaan.
Onko Teillä __ x __ x __ kokoista rengasta?

1. Tarvitsen sisärenkaallisen eturenkaan.
Onko Teillä __ x __ x __ kokoista rengasta?

2. Onko Teillä sisarengasta tälle renkaalle?

3. Tarvitsen sisärenkaallisen takarenkaan.
Onko Teillä __ x __ x __ kokoista rengasta?

4. Voitteko vaihtaa renkaan?

5. Tarvitsen sytystulpat. Onko Teillä tätä mallia?

6. Tarvitsen ilmansuodattimen. Onko Teillä tätä mallia.

7. Tarvitsen polttoaineensuodattimen. Onko Teillä tätä mallia?

KYLLÄ
EI
PALJONKO MAKSAA?
SAATAVILLA NYT HETI?
__ PÄIVIEN KULUTTUA?
__ VIIKKOJEN KULUTTUA?

335

48. I need an oil filter. Do you have this type?

49. Do you have a brake cable?

50. Do you have a choke cable?

51. Do you have a clutch cable?

52. Do you have a speedometer cable?

53. Do you have a throttle cable?

54. Do you have a 10 amp fuse?

55. Do you have a 15 amp fuse?

56. Do you have a main fuse?

57. Do you have starter brushes?

58. Do you have a bus or blade fuse?

59. Do you have an ACG plug?

60. Do you have a head light bulb/globe?

61. Do you have a tail light bulb/globe?

62. Do you have a turn indicator bulb/globe?

63. Do you have instrument bulbs/globes?

64. Do you have valve/rocker cover gaskets?

65. Do you have valve/rocker cover bolt packings?

66. Do you have a chain and sprocket?

67. Do you have a master link/drive chain joint?

FRAME & ENGINE WORDS

68. Alternator/generator

69. Battery

70. Bolt

71. Brake pad

72. Brake shoes

73. Carburetor

YES
NO
HOW MUCH DOES IT COST?
AVAILABLE NOW?
__ DAYS?
__ WEEKS?

48. Tarvitsen öljynsuodattimen. Onko Teillä tätä mallia?
49. Onko Teillä jarruvaijeria?
50. Onko Teillä rikastimen vaijeria?
51. Onko Teillä kytkinvaijeria?
52. Onko Teillä nopeusmittarin vaijeria?
53. Onko Teillä kaasuvaijeria?
54. Onko Teillä 10 A sulaketta?
55. Onko Teillä 15 A sulaketta?
56. Onko Teillä pääsulaketta?
57. Onko Teillä käynnistinmoottorin hiiliä?
58. Onko Teillä putki-tai levysulaketta?
59. Onko Teillä ACG pistoke (laturin pistoke)?
60. Onko Teillä etuvalopolttimo?
61. Onko Teillä takavalon polttimoa?
62. Onko Teillä vilkun polttimoa?
63. Onko Teillä mittarivalon polttimoita?
64. Onko Teillä venttiilikoneiston kannen tiiviste?
65. Onko Teillä venttilikonneiston kannen pulttien tiivisteet?
66. Onko Teillä ketjut ja rattaat?
67. Onko Teillä ketjutlukkoa?

RUNKO JA MOOTTORI SANASTOA

68. Laturi
69. Akku
70. Pultti
71. Jarrupala
72. Jarrukengät
73. Kaasutin

KYLLÄ
EI
PALJONKO MAKSAA?
SAATAVILLA NYT HETI?
__ PÄIVIEN KULUTTUA?
__ VIIKKOJEN KULUTTUA?

74. Chain

75. Clutch

76. Diodes

77. Drive flange

78. Drive line

79. Drive shaft

80. Electrical wire

81. Fuel pump

82. Gear box

83. Lock nut

84. Machine screw

85. Master link/drive chain joint

86. Nut

87. Rectifier

88. Rotor

89. Sheet metal screw

90. Solenoid

91. Starter motor

92. Valve

93. Washer

94. Wheel bearing

95. Wire

YES
NO
HOW MUCH DOES IT COST?
AVAILABLE NOW?
__ DAYS?
__ WEEKS?

FINNISH
(SUOMEKSI)

TRANSLATED BY HONDA OF FINLAND

The
ENDLESS
RIDE

74. Ketju
75. Kytkin
76. Diodeja
77. Vetolaippa
78. Ketjulinja
79. Kardaani/vetoakseli
80. Sähkäjohto
81. Polttoainepumppu
82. Vaihdelaatikko
83. Lukkomutteri
84. Koneruuvi
85. Ketjulukko
86. Mutteri
87. Tasasuuntaaja
88. Roottori
89. Peltimutteri
90. Solenoidi
91. Käynnistinmoottori
92. Venttiili
93. Aluslevy
94. Pyörän laakeri
95. Vaijeri

KYLLÄ
EI
PALJONKO MAKSAA?
SAATAVILLA NYT HETI?
__ PÄIVIEN KULUTTUA?
__ VIIKKOJEN KULUTTUA?

AT THE REFUELING STATION

1. Do you have 95 octane, leaded or 4-Star?
2. Super?
3. Unleaded?
4. Is this the main road to __ ?
5. Will this road go to __ ?
6. To the left
7. Straight ahead
8. To the right
9. Behind
10. Is there a motorcycle repair shop near here?
11. About how many kilometers to __ ?

PARTS & SERVICE

12. I have a dead battery. Do you have jumper cables/jump leads?
13. The Positive (+) Terminal
14. The Negative (-) Terminal
15. Can you charge my battery?
16. Can you please give me a push start/bump start?
17. Do you have distilled water?
18. Do you have a new battery?
19. Can you adjust my valves? My intake is __ , my exhaust is __ .
20. Do you have shims?
21. The engine won't start. Can you check-out the problem?
22. The engine is running rough. Can you check-out the problem?
23. I have an unusual sound in the engine.
    Can you check-out the problem?

YES
NO
HOW MUCH DOES IT COST?
AVAILABLE NOW?
__ DAYS?
__ WEEKS?

NORWEGIAN
(NORSK)

TRANSLATED BY HONDA OF NORWAY

The
ENDLESS
RIDE

PÅ BENSINSTASJONEN

1. Har du 95 oktan?
2. Super?
3. Blyfri?
4. Er dette hovedveien til __ ?
5. Går denne veien til __ ?
6. Til venstre
7. Rett fram
8. Til høyre
9. Bak
10. Er det et motorsykkelverksted i nærheten?
11. Omtrent hvormange km __ ?

DELER & SERVICE

12. Jeg har et flatt batteri. Har du startkabler?
13. Den positive polen (+)
14. Den negative polen (-)
15. Kan du lade batteriet mitt?
16. Kan du være snill å hjelpe meg ogdytte igang?
17. Har du destillert vann?
18. Har du et nytt batteri?
19. Kan du justere ventilene mine?
    Innsugsklaringen er __ , eksosklaringen er __ .
20. Har du de nødvendige (shims)?
21. Motoren vil ikke starte. Kan du sjekke det?
22. Motoren går ikke pent. Kan du sjekke det?
23. Jeg har en unormal lyd i motoren. Kan du sjekke det?

JA
NEI
HVOR MYE KOSTER DET?
ER DE TILGJENGELIGE NÅ?
__ DAGER?
__ UKER?

341

24. I have an unusual sound in the gear box.
Can you check-out the problem?

25. I have an unusual sound in the final drive.
Can you check-out the problem?

26. Can you service my cooling system?

27. Can you change the thermostat?

28. Can you tighten the spokes?

29. Can you service my front brakes?

30. Can you service my rear brakes?

31. Can you change the oil in my motorcycle?

32. Can you fix a puncture?

33. Do you have compressed air?

34. Do you have anti-freeze?

35. Do you have brake/clutch fluid?

36. Do you have 4-stroke engine oil?

37. Do you have 2-stroke engine oil?

38. Do you have octane booster?

39. I need a tubeless type front tire. Do you have a __ x __ x __ tire?

40. I need a tubeless type rear tire. Do you have a __ x __ x __ tire?

41. I need a tube type front tire. Do you have a __ x __ x __ tire?

42. Do you have an inner tube for this tire?

43. I need a tube type rear tire. Do you have a __ x __ x __ tire?

44. Can you change the tire?

45. I need some spark plugs. Do you have this type?

46. I need an air filter. Do you have this type?

47. I need a fuel filter. Do you have this type?

48. I need an oil filter. Do you have this type?

49. Do you have a brake cable?

YES
NO
HOW MUCH DOES IT COST?
AVAILABLE NOW?
__ DAYS?
__ WEEKS?

4. Jeg har en ulyd i gearkassa. Kan du sjekke det?

5. Jeg har en ulyd i kardangen. Kan du sjekke det?

6. Kan du ta en service på kjøle systemet mitt?

7. Kan du skifte termostaten?

8. Kan du stramme eikene?

9. Kan du ta en service på frambremsen min?

0. Kan du ta en service på bakbremsen min?

1. Kan du skifte olje på motorsykkelen min?

2. Kan du reparere en punktering?

3. Har du trykkluft?

4. Har du frostvæske?

5. Har du bremsevæske?

6. Har du 4 takts motorolje?

7. Har du 2 takts motorolje? (injeksjonsolje)

8. Har du octan booster?

9. Jeg trenger et slangeløst fordekk. Har du et __ x __ x __ dekk?

0. Jeg trenger et slangeløst bakdekk. Har du et __ x __ x __dekk?

1. Jeg trenger et fordekk for slange.
Har du et __ x __ x __ dekk?

2. Har du en slange for det dekket?

3. Jeg trenger et bakdekk for slange.
Har du et __ x __ x __ dekk?

4. Kan du legge om (skifte) dekket?

5. Jeg trenger tennplugger. Har du denne typen?

6. Jeg trenger et luftfilter. Har du denne typen?

7. Jeg trenger et bensinfilter. Har du denne typen?

8. Jeg trenger et oljefilter. Har du denne typen?

9. Har du en bremsewire?

JA
NEI
HVOR MYE KOSTER DET?
ER DE TILGJENGELIGE NÅ?
__ DAGER?
__ UKER?

343

50. Do you have a choke cable?

51. Do you have a clutch cable?

52. Do you have a speedometer cable?

53. Do you have a throttle cable?

54. Do you have a 10 amp fuse?

55. Do you have a 15 amp fuse?

56. Do you have a main fuse?

57. Do you have starter brushes?

58. Do you have a bus or blade fuse?

59. Do you have an ACG plug?

60. Do you have a head light bulb/globe?

61. Do you have a tail light bulb/globe?

62. Do you have a turn indicator bulb/globe?

63. Do you have instrument bulbs/globes?

64. Do you have valve/rocker cover gaskets?

65. Do you have valve/rocker cover bolt packings?

66. Do you have a chain and sprocket?

67. Do you have a master link/drive chain joint?

FRAME & ENGINE WORDS

68. Alternator/generator

69. Battery

70. Bolt

71. Brake pad

72. Brake shoes

73. Carburetor

74. Chain

75. Clutch

> *YES*
> *NO*
> *HOW MUCH DOES IT COST?*
> *AVAILABLE NOW?*
> *__ DAYS?*
> *__ WEEKS?*

NORWEGIAN
(NORSK)

TRANSLATED BY HONDA OF NORWAY

The
ENDLESS
RIDE

0. Har du en chokewire?

1. Har du en clutchwire?

2. Har du en speedometerwire?

3. Har du en gasswire?

4. Har du en 10 amp sikring?

5. Har du en 15 amp sikring?

6. Har du en hovedsikring?

7. Har du børster til selvstarter? (kullstifter)

8. Har du en glassikring?

9. Har du en ACG kontakt?

0. Har du en hovedlyspære?

1. Har du en baklyspære?

2. Har du en blinklyspære?

3. Har du pærer til instrumentlys?

4. Har du ventildeksel pakning?

5. Har du pakninger til ventil deksel skruene?

6. Har du kjede og drev?

7. Har du en kjedelås?

RAMME OG MOTORDELER

8. Alternator/generator/dynamo

9. Batteri

0. Bolt

1. Bremsekloss

2. Bremsesko

3. Forgasser

4. Kjede

5. Clutch

JA
NEI
HVOR MYE KOSTER DET?
ER DE TILGJENGELIGE NÅ?
__ DAGER?
__ UKER?

345

The ENDLESS
RIDE

76. Diodes

77. Drive flange

78. Drive line

79. Drive shaft

80. Electrical wire

81. Fuel pump

82. Gear box

83. Lock nut

84. Machine screw

85. Master link/drive chain joint

86. Nut

87. Rectifier

88. Rotor

89. Sheet metal screw

90. Solenoid

91. Starter motor

92. Valve

93. Washer

94. Wheel bearing

95. Wire

YES
NO
HOW MUCH DOES IT COST?
AVAILABLE NOW?
__ DAYS?
__ WEEKS?

NORWEGIAN
(NORSK)

TRANSLATED BY HONDA OF NORWAY

The
ENDLESS
RIDE

6. Dioder
7. Kobling mellom kardang og bakhjul
8. Drivverket
9. Drivaksel
0. Elektrisk ledning
1. Bensinpumpe
2. Gearkasse
3. Låsemutter
4. Maskin skrue
5. Kjedelås
6. Mutter
7. Likeretter
8. Rotor
9. Karosseri skrue
0. Relè
1. Starter motor
2. Ventil
3. Skive
4. Hjullager
5. Ledning

JA
NEI
HVOR MYE KOSTER DET?
ER DE TILGJENGELIGE NÅ?
__ DAGER?
__ UKER?

AT THE REFUELING STATION

1. Do you have 95 octane, leaded or 4-Star?
2. Super?
3. Unleaded?
4. Is this the main road to __ ?
5. Will this road go to __ ?
6. To the left
7. Straight ahead
8. To the right
9. Behind
10. Is there a motorcycle repair shop near here?
11. About how many kilometers to __ ?

PARTS & SERVICE

12. I have a dead battery. Do you have jumper cables/jump leads?
13. The Positive (+) Terminal
14. The Negative (-) Terminal
15. Can you charge my battery?
16. Can you please give me a push start/bump start?
17. Do you have distilled water?
18. Do you have a new battery?
19. Can you adjust my valves? My intake is __ , my exhaust is __ .
20. Do you have shims?
21. The engine won't start. Can you check-out the problem?
22. The engine is running rough. Can you check-out the problem?
23. I have an unusual sound in the engine.
    Can you check-out the problem?

YES
NO
HOW MUCH DOES IT COST?
AVAILABLE NOW?
__ DAYS?
__ WEEKS?

PÅ BENSINSTATIONEN

1. Har Ni 95 oktans bensin?

2. Högoktanig bensin?

3. Oblyad? (blyfri?)

4. Är detta huvudvägen till __ ?

5. Går denna vägen till __ ?

6. Till vänster

7. Rakt fram

8. Till höger

9. Bakom

10. Finns det någon motorcykelverkstad i närheten?

11. Hur många kilometer __ ?

DELAR OCH SERVICE

12. Jag har ett dött batteri. Har Ni startkablar?

13. Pluspolen (+)

14. Minuspolen (-)

15. Kan Ni ladda mitt batteri?

16. Var snäll och skjut igång mig?

17. Har Ni destillerat vatten?

18. Har Ni ett nytt batteri?

19. Kan Ni justera ventilerna? Spel på insug __ , spel på avgas __ .

20. Har Ni shims?

21. Motorn startar inte. Kan Ni kontrollera felet?

22. Motorn går ojämnt. Kan Ni kontrollera det?

23. Jag har ett ovanligt ljud i motorn. Kan Ni kontrollera detta?

JA
NEJ
HUR MYCKET KOSTAR DET?
HAR NI DET (HEMMA)?
__ HUR MÅNGA DAGAR TAR DET?
__ HUR MÅNGA VECKOR TAR DET?

349

24. I have an unusual sound in the gear box.
Can you check-out the problem?

25. I have an unusual sound in the final drive.
Can you check-out the problem?

26. Can you service my cooling system?

27. Can you change the thermostat?

28. Can you tighten the spokes?

29. Can you service my front brakes?

30. Can you service my rear brakes?

31. Can you change the oil in my motorcycle?

32. Can you fix a puncture?

33. Do you have compressed air?

34. Do you have anti-freeze?

35. Do you have brake/clutch fluid?

36. Do you have 4-stroke engine oil?

37. Do you have 2-stroke engine oil?

38. Do you have octane booster?

39. I need a tubeless type front tire. Do you have a __ x __ x __ tire?

40. I need a tubeless type rear tire. Do you have a __ x __ x __ tire?

41. I need a tube type front tire. Do you have a __ x __ x __ tire?

42. Do you have an inner tube for this tire?

43. I need a tube type rear tire. Do you have a __ x __ x __ tire?

44. Can you change the tire?

45. I need some spark plugs. Do you have this type?

46. I need an air filter. Do you have this type?

47. I need a fuel filter. Do you have this type?

48. I need an oil filter. Do you have this type?

49. Do you have a brake cable?

YES
NO
HOW MUCH DOES IT COST?
AVAILABLE NOW?
__ DAYS?
__ WEEKS?

4. Jag har ett ovanligt ljud i växellådan. Kan Ni kontrollera det?

5. Jag har ett ovanligt ljud i slutväxeln. Kan Ni kontrollera det?

6. Kan Ni reparera kylsystemet?

7. Kan Ni byta termostat?

8. Kan Ni dra åt ekrarna?

9. Kan Ni se över frambromsen?

0. Kan Ni kontrollera min bakbroms?

1. Kan Ni byta olja i min motorcykel?

2. Kan Ni laga en punktering?

3. Har Ni tryckluft?

4. Har Ni kylarvätska?

5. Har Ni bromsolja?

6. Har Ni motorolja för 4-takt?

7. Har Ni tvåtaktsolja?

8. Har Ni oktanhöjande tillsatsmedel?

9. Jag behöver ett slanglöst fram däck. Har Ni ett __ x __ x __ däck?

0. Jag behöver ett slanglöst bakdäck. Har Ni ett __ x __ x __ däck?

1. Jag behöver ett framdäck för slang.
   Har Ni ett __ x __ x __ däck?

2. Har Ni en slang för detta däck?

3. Jag behöver ett bakdäck för slang.
   Har Ni ett __ x __ x __ bakdäck?

4. Kan Ni byta däck?

5. Jag behöver några tändstift. Har Ni denna typ?

6. Jag behöver ett luftfilter. Har Ni denna typ?

7. Jag behöver ett bränslefilter. Har Ni denna typ?

8. Jag behöver ett oljefilter. Har Ni denna typ?

9. Har Ni en bromsvajer?

JA
NEJ
HUR MYCKET KOSTAR DET?
HAR NI DET (HEMMA)?
__ HUR MÅNGA DAGAR TAR DET?
__ HUR MÅNGA VECKOR TAR DET?

351

50. Do you have a choke cable?

51. Do you have a clutch cable?

52. Do you have a speedometer cable?

53. Do you have a throttle cable?

54. Do you have a 10 amp fuse?

55. Do you have a 15 amp fuse?

56. Do you have a main fuse?

57. Do you have starter brushes?

58. Do you have a bus or blade fuse?

59. Do you have an ACG plug?

60. Do you have a head light bulb/globe?

61. Do you have a tail light bulb/globe?

62. Do you have a turn indicator bulb/globe?

63. Do you have instrument bulbs/globes?

64. Do you have valve/rocker cover gaskets?

65. Do you have valve/rocker cover bolt packings?

66. Do you have a chain and sprocket?

67. Do you have a master link/drive chain joint?

FRAME & ENGINE WORDS

68. Alternator/generator

69. Battery

70. Bolt

71. Brake pad

72. Brake shoes

73. Carburetor

74. Chain

75. Clutch

YES
NO
HOW MUCH DOES IT COST?
AVAILABLE NOW?
__ DAYS?
__ WEEKS?

SWEDISH
(SVENSKA)

TRANSLATED BY HONDA OF SWEDEN

The
ENDLESS
RIDE

0. Har Ni en chokevajer?

1. Har Ni en kopplingsvajer?

2. Har Ni en hastighetsmätarvajer?

3. Har Ni en gasvajer?

4. Har Ni en 10 Amp. säkring?

5. Har Ni en 15 Amp. säkring?

6. Har Ni en huvudsäkring?

7. Har Ni kol till startmotorn?

8. Har Ni säkringar?

9. Har Ni en koppling för generatorkablarna?

0. Har Ni en glödlampa för hel-och halvljus?

1. Har Ni en glödlampa till bakljuset?

2. Har Ni en glödlampa till blinkersindikatorn?

3. Har Ni glödlampor till instrumentbelysningen?

4. Har Ni packningar till ventilkåpan?

5. Har Ni tändningar till bultarna för ventilkåpan?

6. Har Ni en kedja och drev?

7. Har Ni ett kedjelås?

RAM-OCH MOTORUTTRYCK

8. Generator

9. Batteri

0. Bult

1. Bromspad

2. Bromsback

3. Förgasare

4. Kedja

5. Koppling

JA
NEJ
HUR MYCKET KOSTAR DET?
HAR NI DET (HEMMA)?
__ HUR MÅNGA DAGAR TAR DET?
__ HUR MÅNGA VECKOR TAR DET?

76. Diodes
77. Drive flange
78. Drive line
79. Drive shaft
80. Electrical wire
81. Fuel pump
82. Gear box
83. Lock nut
84. Machine screw
85. Master link/drive chain joint
86. Nut
87. Rectifier
88. Rotor
89. Sheet metal screw
90. Solenoid
91. Starter motor
92. Valve
93. Washer
94. Wheel bearing
95. Wire

YES
NO
HOW MUCH DOES IT COST?
AVAILABLE NOW?
__ DAYS?
__ WEEKS?

SWEDISH
(SVENSKA)

TRANSLATED BY HONDA OF SWEDEN

The
ENDLESS
RIDE

76. Diod (-er)
77. Medbringare
78. -
79. Kardan
80. Kabel
81. Bränslepump
82. Växellåda
83. Låsmutter
84. Bult, skruv
85. Kedjelås
86. Mutter
87. Likriktare
88. Rotor (Ankare)
89. Plåtskruv
90. Solenoid (startrelä)
91. Startmotor
92. Ventil
93. Bricka
94. Hjullager
95. Vajer (wire)

JA
NEJ
HUR MYCKET KOSTAR DET?
HAR NI DET (HEMMA)?
__ HUR MÅNGA DAGAR TAR DET?
__ HUR MÅNGA VECKOR TAR DET?

AT THE REFUELING STATION

1. Do you have 95 octane, leaded or 4-Star?
2. Super?
3. Unleaded?
4. Is this the main road to __ ?
5. Will this road go to __ ?
6. To the left
7. Straight ahead
8. To the right
9. Behind
10. Is there a motorcycle repair shop near here?
11. About how many kilometers to __ ?

PARTS & SERVICE

12. I have a dead battery. Do you have jumper cables/jump leads?
13. The Positive (+) Terminal
14. The Negative (-) Terminal
15. Can you charge my battery?
16. Can you please give me a push start/bump start?
17. Do you have distilled water?
18. Do you have a new battery?
19. Can you adjust my valves? My intake is __ , my exhaust is __ .
20. Do you have shims?
21. The engine won't start. Can you check-out the problem?
22. The engine is running rough. Can you check-out the problem?

YES
NO
HOW MUCH DOES IT COST?
AVAILABLE NOW?
__ DAYS?
__ WEEKS?

فـي محطـة البنـزيـن

1. – هل لديكم بنزين بدرجة اوكتين ٩٠/٩١؟
2. – هل لديكم بنزين سوبر؟
3. – هل لديكم بنزين خالي من الرصاص؟
4. – هل هذا هو الطريق الرئيسي المؤدّي إلى .... ؟
5. – هل يؤدّي هذا الطريق الى .... ؟
6. – الى اليسار.
7. – الى الامام.
8. – الى اليمين.
9. – الى الخلف.
10. – هل توجد ورشة لتصليح الموتوسيكلات بالقرب من هنا؟
11. – على بعدُ كم كيلومتر من هنا؟

قطـع الغيـار والتصليـح

12. – البطارية فاضية. هل لديكم كبل عبور وتخط؟
13. – الطرف الموجب (+).
14. – الطرف السالب (–).
15. – هل يمكنكم شحن البطارية؟
16. – هل يمكن دفعي حتى يبدأ المحرّك؟
17. – هل عندكم ماء مقطّر؟
18. – هل عندكم بطارية جديّدة؟
19. – هل يمكنكم ضبط الصمامات؟
    معدل صمام السحب هو .... وصمام العادم هو ....
20. – هل عندكم رقائق ضبط؟
21. – المحرّك لا يبدأ الدوران. هل يمكنكم تحرّي السبب؟
22. – المحرّك يدور باضطراب. هل يمكنكم تحرّي السبب؟

نعم
لا
بكم؟ (ما هو السعر)؟
أموجود الآن؟
أموجود بعد ـــــــ يوم؟
أموجود بعد ـــــــ اسبوع ؟

357

23. I have an unusual sound in the engine.
Can you check-out the problem?

24. I have an unusual sound in the gear box.
Can you check-out the problem?

25. I have an unusual sound in the final drive.
Can you check-out the problem?

26. Can you service my cooling system?

27. Can you change the thermostat?

28. Can you tighten the spokes?

29. Can you service my front brakes?

30. Can you service my rear brakes?

31. Can you change the oil in my motorcycle?

32. Can you fix a puncture?

33. Do you have compressed air?

34. Do you have anti-freeze?

35. Do you have brake/clutch fluid?

36. Do you have 4-stroke engine oil?

37. Do you have 2-stroke engine oil?

38. Do you have octane booster?

39. I need a tubeless type front tire. Do you have a __ x __ x __ tire?

40. I need a tubeless type rear tire. Do you have a __ x __ x __ tire?

41. I need a tube type front tire. Do you have a __ x __ x __ tire?

42. Do you have an inner tube for this tire?

43. I need a tube type rear tire. Do you have a __ x __ x __ tire?

44. Can you change the tire?

45. I need some spark plugs. Do you have this type?

46. I need an air filter. Do you have this type?

YES
NO
HOW MUCH DOES IT COST?
AVAILABLE NOW?
__ DAYS?
__ WEEKS?

ARABIC
(اللغة العربية)

TRANSLATED BY HONDA OF MOROCCO

RIDE
The
ENDLESS

23. ‐ المحرّك يصدر اصواتاً غير عادية.
هل يمكنكم تحرّي السبب؟

24. ‐ توجد اصوات غير عادية في علبة التروس.
هل يمكنكم تحرّي السبب؟

25. ‐ توجد اصوات غير عادية في ناقل الحركة النهائي.
هل يمكنكم تحرّي السبب؟

26. ‐ هل يمكنكم فحص وخدمة نظام التبريد؟

27. ‐ هل يمكنكم تغيير الترموستات؟

28. ‐ هل يمكنكم احكام ربط اسلاك العجلة؟

29. ‐ هل يمكنكم فحص وخدمة الفرامل الأمامية؟

30. ‐ هل يمكنكم فحص وخدمة الفرامل الخلفية؟

31. ‐ هل يمكنكم تغيير زيت الموتوسيكل؟

32. ‐ هل يمكنكم تصليح كاوتش العجلة؟

33. ‐ هل لديكم هواء مضغوط لنفخ العجل؟

34. ‐ هل لديكم سائل مقاوم للتجمّد؟

35. ‐ هل لديكم زيت فرامل وزيت كلاتش؟

36. ‐ هل لديكم زيت محرّكات رباعية الاشواط؟

37. ‐ هل لديكم زيت محرّكات ثنائية الشوط؟

38. ‐ هل لديكم معزز أوكتيني؟

39. ‐ أريد عجلة أمامية بدون اطار داخلي؟
هل لديكم عجلة أمامية بدون اطار داخلي؟

40. ‐ اريد عجلة خلفية بدون اطار داخلي. هل لديكم عجلة خلفية بدون اطار داخلي؟

41. ‐ اريد عجلة أمامية باطار داخلي. هل لديكم عجلة أمامية باطار داخلي؟

42. ‐ هل عندكم اطار داخلي لهذه العجلة؟

43. ‐ اريد عجلة خلفية باطار داخلي. هل لديكم عجلة خلفية باطار داخلي؟

44. ‐ هل يمكنكم تغيير العجلة؟

45. ‐ اريد شمعات اشتعال. هل عندكم هذا النوع؟

46. ‐ اريد مرشح هواء. هل عندكم هذا النوع؟

نعم

لا

بكم؟ (ما هو السعر)؟

أموجود الآن؟

أموجود بعد ـــــــ يوم؟

أموجود بعد ـــــــ اسبوع ؟

47. I need a fuel filter. Do you have this type?

48. I need an oil filter. Do you have this type?

49. Do you have a brake cable?

50. Do you have a choke cable?

51. Do you have a clutch cable?

52. Do you have a speedometer cable?

53. Do you have a throttle cable?

54. Do you have a 10 amp fuse?

55. Do you have a 15 amp fuse?

56. Do you have a main fuse?

57. Do you have starter brushes?

58. Do you have a bus or blade fuse?

59. Do you have an ACG plug?

60. Do you have a head light bulb/globe?

61. Do you have a tail light bulb/globe?

62. Do you have a turn indicator bulb/globe?

63. Do you have instrument bulbs/globes?

64. Do you have valve/rocker cover gaskets?

65. Do you have valve/rocker cover bolt packings?

66. Do you have a chain and sprocket?

67. Do you have a master link/drive chain joint?

FRAME & ENGINE WORDS

68. Alternator/generator

69. Battery

70. Bolt

71. Brake pad

72. Brake shoes

YES
NO
HOW MUCH DOES IT COST?
AVAILABLE NOW?
__ DAYS?
__ WEEKS?

47. – اريد مرشح وقود. هل عندكم هذا النوع؟.
48. – اريد مرشح زيت. هل عندكم هذا النوع؟
49. – هل عندكم كبل فرامل؟
50. – هل عندكم كبل لملف الخنق؟
51. – هل عندكم كبل للكلتش؟
52. – هل عندكم كبل لعداد السرعة؟
53. – هل عندكم كبل للصمام الخانق؟
54. – هل عندكم فيوز ١٠ أمبير؟
55. – هل عندكم فيوز ١٥ أمبير؟
56. – هل عندكم فيوز رئيسي؟
57. – هل عندكم فرجون لبادىء الحركة؟
58. – هل عندكم فيوز لقضيب التوصيل او لريشة المفتاح؟
59. – هل عندكم قابس لجهاز التحكم الاوتوماتيكي؟
60. – هل عندكم مصباح للاضاءة الأمامية؟
61. – هل عندكم بصيلة للاضاءة الخلفية الحمراء؟
62. – هل عندكم مصباح لمؤشر الدوران؟
63. – هل عندكم بصيلات لانارة لوحة العدادات؟
64. – هل عندكم طوق لمنع التسرّب في غطاء الصمامات؟
65. – هل عندكم مانع تسرّب لغطاء الصمامات؟
66. – هل عندكم سلسلة ووحدة تروس؟
67. – هل عندكم وصلة رئيسية؟

مصطلحات خاصة بالهيكل والمحرّك

68. – المنوّب / المولّد
69. – البطارية
70. – مسمار
71. – وسادة الفرامل
72. – لقمة الفرامل

نعم

لا

بكم؟ (ما هو السعر)؟

أموجود الآن؟

أموجود بعد ـــــ يوم؟

أموجود بعد ـــــ اسبوع ؟

73. Carburetor

74. Chain

75. Clutch

76. Diodes

77. Drive flange

78. Drive line

79. Drive shaft

80. Electrical wire

81. Fuel pump

82. Gear box

83. Lock nut

84. Machine screw

85. Master link/drive chain joint

86. Nut

87. Rectifier

88. Rotor

89. Sheet metal screw

90. Solenoid

91. Starter motor

92. Valve

93. Washer

94. Wheel bearing

95. Wire

The
ENDLESS
RIDE

YES
NO
HOW MUCH DOES IT COST?
AVAILABLE NOW?
__ DAYS?
__ WEEKS?

ARABIC
(اللغة العربية)

TRANSLATED BY HONDA OF MOROCCO

The
ENDLESS
RIDE

73. – الكربوريتور
74. – السلسلة
75. – الكلاتش
76. – الدايود
77. – شفة ناقل الحركة
78. – خط الادارة
79. – عمواد الادارة
80. – الاسلاك الكهربائية
81. – مضخة الوقود
82. – علبة التروس
83. – صمولة زنق
84. – مسمار ربط ملولب
85. – الوصلة الرئيسية
86. – صمولة
87. – المقوِّم
88. – العضو الدوّار
89. – مسمار صفيح
90. – الملف اللولبي
91. – موتور بدء الحركة
92. – الصمام
93. – الفلكة (الوردة)
94. – محامل العجلات
95. – السلك

نعم

لا

بكم؟ (ما هو السعر)؟

أموجود الآن؟

أموجود بعد ــــــ يوم؟

أموجود بعد ــــــ اسبوع ؟

AT THE REFUELING STATION

1. Do you have 95 octane, leaded or 4-Star?
2. Super?
3. Unleaded?
4. Is this the main road to __ ?
5. Will this road go to __ ?
6. To the left
7. Straight ahead
8. To the right
9. Behind
10. Is there a motorcycle repair shop near here?
11. About how many kilometers to __ ?

PARTS & SERVICE

12. I have a dead battery. Do you have jumper cables/jump leads?
13. The Positive (+) Terminal
14. The Negative (-) Terminal
15. Can you charge my battery?
16. Can you please give me a push start/bump start?
17. Do you have distilled water?
18. Do you have a new battery?
19. Can you adjust my valves? My intake is __ , my exhaust is __ .
20. Do you have shims?
21. The engine won't start. Can you check-out the problem?
22. The engine is running rough. Can you check-out the problem?
23. I have an unusual sound in the engine.
    Can you check-out the problem?

YES
NO
HOW MUCH DOES IT COST?
AVAILABLE NOW?
__ DAYS?
__ WEEKS?

PETROL PUMP KE PAAS

1. KIYA AAP KE PASS 91 OCTANE HAI
2. SUPER
3. UNLEADED
4. KIYA YEH MUKHIYA SARAK __ KO JATI HAI
5. KIYA YEH SARAK __ KO JAYE GI
6. BAAIN TARAF
7. SIDHAA
8. DAAIN TARAF
9. PEECHAY KI TARAF
10. KIYA YAHAN PAR KOI MOTORCYCLE THEEK KARNE KI DUKAAN HAI
11. LAGHBAGH KITNE __ KMS

PARTS & SERVICE

12. MERE PASS DEAD BATTERY HAI KIYA APP KE PASS JUMPER CABLE MIL SAKTI HAI
13. THE POSITIVE (+) TERMINAL HAI
14. THE NEGATIVE (-) TERMINAL HAI
15. KIYA AAP MERI BATTERY CHARGE KAR SAKTE HAI
16. KIYA AAP MUJHE PUSH START DE SAKTE HAIN
17. KIYA AAP KE PASS DISTILLED WATER HAIN
18. KIYA AAP KE PASS NAI BATTERY HAI
19. KIYA AAP VALVE ADJUST KAR SAKTE HAIN
20. KIYA AAP KE SHIMS HAI
21. ENGINE START NAHIN HUA. KIYA AAP MUSHKIL BATTA SAKTE HAIN
22. ENGINE THEEK NAHIN CHAL RAHA KIYA AAP BTTA SAKTEN HAIN
23. ENGINE SAI KOI ANOKHI AWWAAZ AA RAHI HAI. KIYA AAP PTTA LAGA SAKTE HAIN

HAAN
NAHIN
YEH KITNE KA HAI
ABHI HAI
__ KITNE DIN KE BAAD
__ KITNE SAPTAH KE BAAD

24. I have an unusual sound in the gear box.
Can you check-out the problem?

25. I have an unusual sound in the final drive.
Can you check-out the problem?

26. Can you service my cooling system?

27. Can you change the thermostat?

28. Can you tighten the spokes?

29. Can you service my front brakes?

30. Can you service my rear brakes?

31. Can you change the oil in my motorcycle?

32. Can you fix a puncture?

33. Do you have compressed air?

34. Do you have anti-freeze?

35. Do you have brake/clutch fluid?

36. Do you have 4-stroke engine oil?

37. Do you have 2-stroke engine oil?

38. Do you have octane booster?

39. I need a tubeless type front tire. Do you have a __ x __ x __ tire?

40. I need a tubeless type rear tire.
Do you have a __ x __ x __ tire?

41. I need a tube type front tire.
Do you have a __ x __ x __ tire?

42. Do you have an inner tube for this tire?

43. I need a tube type rear tire.
Do you have a __ x __ x __ tire?

44. Can you change the tire?

45. I need some spark plugs. Do you have this type?

46. I need an air filter. Do you have this type?

47. I need a fuel filter. Do you have this type?

YES
NO
HOW MUCH DOES IT COST?
AVAILABLE NOW?
__ DAYS?
__ WEEKS?

HINDI
(AS SPOKEN IN INDIA)

TRANSLATED BY HONDA OF INDIA

The
ENDLESS
RIDE

4. GEAR BOX MAIN KOI AZIB AWAZ AA RAHI HAI KIYA AAP BATTA SAKTE HAIN

5. FINAL DRIVE MAIN AZIB AWWAZ AA RAHI HAI KIYA AAP PATA LAGA SAKTE HAIN

6. COOLING SYSTEM KI SERVICE KAR SAKTE HAIN

7. KIYA AAP THERMOSTAT BADAL SAKTE HAIN

8. KIYA AAP SPOKES KAS SAKTE HAIN

9. MERE AGLE BRAKES SERVICE KAR SAKTE HAIN

0. KIYA APP MERI PEESHAY KI BRAKES THEEK KAR SAKTE HAIN

1. KIYA AAP MOTORCYCLE MAIN TEL BADAL SAKTE HAIN

2. KIYA AAP PUNCHER LAGGA SAKTE HAIN

3. COMPRESSED HAWA HAI

4. ANTI FREEZE HAI

5. KIYA AAP KE PASS BRAKE/CLUTCH FLUID HAI

6. 4 STROKE ENGINE TEL HAI

7. 2 STROKE ENGINE TEL HAI

8. OCTANE BOOSTER HAI

9. MUJHE BINA TUBE KE AGLA TYRE CHAHIYA. KIYA AAP KE PASS ___ HAI

0. PEESHAY BALA BINA TUBE KE TYRE CHAHIYA. KIYA AAP KE PASS ___ HAI

1. KIYA AAP KE PASS TUBE WALA AGLA TYRE HAI. KIYA AAP KE PASS ___ TYRE HAI

2. IS TYRE KI TUBE HAI

3. TUBE TYRE PISHLA WALA CHAHIYA KIYA AAP KE PASS __ TYRE HAI

4. KIYA AAP TYRE BADAL SAKTE HAIN

5. MUJHE SPARK PLUGS CHAHIYA. KIYA AAP KE PASS IS TARAH KA HAI

6. MUJHE AIR FILTER CHAHIYA. KIYA AAP KE PASS YEH WALI KISM HAI

7. MUJHE FUEL FILTER CHAHYA. KIYA AAP KE PASS IS TARAH KA HAI

HAAN
NAHIN
YEH KITNE KA HAI
ABHI HAI
__ KITNE DIN KE BAAD
__ KITNE SAPTAH KE BAAD

48. I need an oil filter. Do you have this type?

49. Do you have a brake cable?

50. Do you have a choke cable?

51. Do you have a clutch cable?

52. Do you have a speedometer cable?

53. Do you have a throttle cable?

54. Do you have a 10 amp fuse?

55. Do you have a 15 amp fuse?

56. Do you have a main fuse?

57. Do you have starter brushes?

58. Do you have a bus or blade fuse?

59. Do you have an ACG plug?

60. Do you have a head light bulb/globe?

61. Do you have a tail light bulb/globe?

62. Do you have a turn indicator bulb/globe?

63. Do you have instrument bulbs/globes?

64. Do you have valve/rocker cover gaskets?

65. Do you have valve/rocker cover bolt packings?

66. Do you have a chain and sprocket?

67. Do you have a master link/drive chain joint?

FRAME & ENGINE WORDS

68. Alternator/generator

69. Battery

70. Bolt

71. Brake pad

72. Brake shoes

73. Carburetor

YES
NO
HOW MUCH DOES IT COST?
AVAILABLE NOW?
__ DAYS?
__ WEEKS?

48. MUJHE OIL FILTER CHAHIYA. KLIYA AAP KE PASS IS TARAH KA HAI

49. AAP KE PASS BRAKE CABLE HAI

50. AAP KE PASS CHOKE CABLE HAI

51. AAP KE PASS CLUTCH CABLE HAI

52. AAP KE PASS SPEEDOMETER CABLE HAI

53. AAP KE PASS THROTTLE CABLE HAI

54. 10 AMPS KA FUSE HAI

55. 15 AMPS KA FUSE HAI

56. MAIN FUSE HAI

57. KIYA AAP KE PASS STARTER BRUSHES HAI

58. KIYA AAP KE PASS BUS OR BLADE FUSE HAI

59. KIYA AAP KE PASS ACG PLUG HAI

60. KIYA AAP KE PASS HEAD LIGHT BULB/GLOBE HAI

61. KIYA PEESHAY KA BULB/GLOBE HAI

62. KIYA TURN INDICATOR BULB/GLOBE HAI

63. KIYA AAP KE PASS INSTRUMENT BULB/GLOBE HAI

64. KIYA VALVE/ROCKER COVER GASKETS HAI

65. KIYA AAP KE PASS VALVE COVER BOLT PACKING HAI

66. KIYA AAP KE PASS CHAIN AUR SPROCKET HAI

67. KIYA AAP KE PASS MASTER LINK HAI

FRAME & ENGINE WORDS

68. ALTERNATOR/GENERATOR HAI

69. BATTERY HAI

70. BOLT HAI

71. BRAKE PAD HAI

72. BRAKE SHOE HAI

73. CARBURETOR HAI

HAAN
NAHIN
YEH KITNE KA HAI
ABHI HAI
__ KITNE DIN KE BAAD
__ KITNE SAPTAH KE BAAD

74. Chain

75. Clutch

76. Diodes

77. Drive flange

78. Drive line

79. Drive shaft

80. Electrical wire

81. Fuel pump

82. Gear box

83. Lock nut

84. Machine screw

85. Master link/drive chain joint

86. Nut

87. Rectifier

88. Rotor

89. Sheet metal screw

90. Solenoid

91. Starter motor

92. Valve

93. Washer

94. Wheel bearing

95. Wire

YES
NO
HOW MUCH DOES IT COST?
AVAILABLE NOW?
__ DAYS?
__ WEEKS?

4. CHAIN HAI

5. CLUTCH HAI

6. DIODES HAI

7. DRIVE FLANGE HAI

8. DRIVE LINE HAI

9. DRIVE SHAFT HAI

0. ELECTRICAL WIRE HAI

1. FUEL PUMP HAI

2. GEAR BOX HAI

3. LOCK NUT HAI

4. MACHINE SCREW HAI

5. MASTER LINK/DRIVE CHAIN JOINT HAI

6. NUT HAI

7. RECTIFIER HAI

8. ROTOR HAI

9. SHEET METAL SCREW HAI

0. SOLENOID HAI

1. STARTER MOTOR HAI

2. VALVE HAI

3. WASHER HAI

4. WHEEL BEARING HAI

5. WIRE HAI

HAAN
NAHIN
YEH KITNE KA HAI
ABHI HAI
__ KITNE DIN KE BAAD
__ KITNE SAPTAH KE BAAD

AT THE REFUELING STATION

1. Do you have 95 octane, leaded or 4-Star?
2. Super?
3. Unleaded?
4. Is this the main road to __ ?
5. Will this road go to __ ?
6. To the left
7. Straight ahead
8. To the right
9. Behind
10. Is there a motorcycle repair shop near here?
11. About how many kilometers to __ ?

PARTS & SERVICE

12. I have a dead battery. Do you have jumper cables/jump leads?
13. The Positive (+) Terminal
14. The Negative (-) Terminal
15. Can you charge my battery?
16. Can you please give me a push start/bump start?
17. Do you have distilled water?
18. Do you have a new battery?
19. Can you adjust my valves? My intake is __ , my exhaust is __ .
20. Do you have shims?
21. The engine won't start. Can you check-out the problem?

YES
NO
HOW MUCH DOES IT COST?
AVAILABLE NOW?
__ DAYS?
__ WEEKS?

在加油站

1. 你有辛烷值90/91的汽油嗎？

2. 超級？

3. 無鉛？

4. 這是不是去 ＿＿＿ 的一條主要公路？

5. 這一條公路是去 ＿＿＿ ？

6. 向左

7. 向前直走

8. 向右

9. 後面

10. 附近有機車修理店嗎？

11. 大約有幾公里 ＿＿＿ ？

零件與服務

12. 我的電池壞了。你有沒有接電池的電線？

13.（＋）正電極

14.（－）負電極

15. 你能爲我的電池充電嗎？

16. 你能不能幫我推車使引擎發動嗎？

17. 你有沒有蒸餾水？

18. 你有沒有新的電池嗎？

19. 你能調整閥門嗎？我的進氣閥門是 ＿＿＿ ，出氣閥門是 ＿＿＿ 。

20. 你有沒有填隙片嗎？

21. 引擎無法發動, 你能檢查出是什麼問題嗎？

是

不是

多少錢？

現在有嗎？

＿＿＿天？

＿＿＿星期？

The ENDLESS RIDE

22. The engine is running rough. Can you check-out the problem?

23. I have an unusual sound in the engine.
Can you check-out the problem?

24. I have an unusual sound in the gear box.
Can you check-out the problem?

25. I have an unusual sound in the final drive.
Can you check-out the problem?

26. Can you service my cooling system?

27. Can you change the thermostat?

28. Can you tighten the spokes?

29. Can you service my front brakes?

30. Can you service my rear brakes?

31. Can you change the oil in my motorcycle?

32. Can you fix a puncture?

33. Do you have compressed air?

34. Do you have anti-freeze?

35. Do you have brake/clutch fluid?

36. Do you have 4-stroke engine oil?

37. Do you have 2-stroke engine oil?

38. Do you have octane booster?

39. I need a tubeless type front tire. Do you have a __ x __ x __ tire?

40. I need a tubeless type rear tire. Do you have a __ x __ x __ tire?

41. I need a tube type front tire. Do you have a __ x __ x __ tire?

42. Do you have an inner tube for this tire?

43. I need a tube type rear tire. Do you have a __ x __ x __ tire?

44. Can you change the tire?

45. I need some spark plugs. Do you have this type?

YES
NO
HOW MUCH DOES IT COST?
AVAILABLE NOW?
__ DAYS?
__ WEEKS?

The ENDLESS RIDE

22. 引擎的噪音很大，你能檢查出是什麼問題嗎？

23. 我覺得引擎的聲音很怪，你能檢查出是什麼問題嗎？

24. 我覺得在齒輪箱有噪音，你能檢查出是什麼問題嗎？

25. 我覺得終端傳速組件有奇異的聲音，你能檢查出是什麼問題嗎？

26. 你能替我檢查冷却系統嗎？

27. 能換掉恒温器嗎？

28. 能上緊輪輻嗎？

29. 能替我檢修前面的刹車嗎？

30. 能替我檢修後面的刹車嗎？

31. 能替我的機車換潤滑油嗎？

32. 能替我補刺破的輪胎嗎？

33. 你有空氣壓縮機嗎？

34. 你有防凍劑嗎？

35. 你有刹車及離合器油嗎？

36. 你有四衝程的機油嗎？

37. 你有二衝程的機油嗎？

38. 你有辛烷的昇壓劑嗎？

39. 我要一條前輪用無內胎的輪胎，你有＿＿ × ＿＿ × ＿＿ 這樣的 尺寸嗎？

40. 我要一條後輪用無內胎的輪胎。你有＿＿ × ＿＿ × ＿＿ × ＿＿ 尺寸嗎？

41. 我要一條前輪用有內胎的輪胎。你有＿＿ × ＿＿ × ＿＿ 這樣的 尺寸嗎？

42. 你有用於這個輪胎的內胎嗎？

43. 我要一條後輪用有內胎的輪胎。你有＿＿ × ＿＿ × ＿＿ 這樣的 尺寸嗎？

44. 你可以替我換輪胎嗎？

45. 我要一些像這樣的火星塞。你有嗎？

是

不是

多少錢？

現在有嗎？

＿＿ 天？

＿＿ 星期？

46. I need an air filter. Do you have this type?

47. I need a fuel filter. Do you have this type?

48. I need an oil filter. Do you have this type?

49. Do you have a brake cable?

50. Do you have a choke cable?

51. Do you have a clutch cable?

52. Do you have a speedometer cable?

53. Do you have a throttle cable?

54. Do you have a 10 amp fuse?

55. Do you have a 15 amp fuse?

56. Do you have a main fuse?

57. Do you have starter brushes?

58. Do you have a bus or blade fuse?

59. Do you have an ACG plug?

60. Do you have a head light bulb/globe?

61. Do you have a tail light bulb/globe?

62. Do you have a turn indicator bulb/globe?

63. Do you have instrument bulbs/globes?

64. Do you have valve/rocker cover gaskets?

65. Do you have valve/rocker cover bolt packings?

66. Do you have a chain and sprocket?

67. Do you have a master link/drive chain joint?

FRAME & ENGINE WORDS

68. Alternator/generator

69. Battery

70. Bolt

71. Brake pad

YES
NO
HOW MUCH DOES IT COST?
AVAILABLE NOW?
__ DAYS?
__ WEEKS?

6. 我要一個空氣濾清器。你有這種型式的嗎？
7. 我要一個汽油濾清器。你有這種型式嗎？
8. 我要一個機油濾清器。你有這種型式嗎？
9. 你有刹車操縱纜？
0. 你有空氣阻塞片操縱纜嗎？
1. 你有離合器操縱纜嗎？
2. 你有速度錶連接纜嗎？
3. 你有汽門操縱纜嗎？
4. 你有10安培的保險絲嗎？
5. 你有15安培的保險絲嗎？
6. 你有主要的保險絲嗎？
7. 你有啓動電機的電刷嗎？
8. 你有主導線或是單式保險絲嗎？
9. 你有 ACG 型的火星塞嗎？
0. 你有車前燈嗎？
1. 你有車尾燈的燈泡嗎？
2. 你有方向燈的燈泡嗎？
3. 你有儀表燈的燈泡嗎？
4. 你有閥門蓋的墊片嗎？
5. 你有閥門蓋螺栓的墊圈嗎？
6. 你有傳動鏈及扣鏈齒輪嗎？
7. 你有主要的鏈環嗎？

車體和引擎名詞

8. 發電機
9. 蓄電池
0. 螺栓
1. 刹車片

是
不是
多少錢？
現在有嗎？
＿＿＿天？
＿＿＿星期？

72. Brake shoes
73. Carburetor
74. Chain
75. Clutch
76. Diodes
77. Drive flange
78. Drive line
79. Drive shaft
80. Electrical wire
81. Fuel pump
82. Gear box
83. Lock nut
84. Machine screw
85. Master link/drive chain joint
86. Nut
87. Rectifier
88. Rotor
89. Sheet metal screw
90. Solenoid
91. Starter motor
92. Valve
93. Washer
94. Wheel bearing
95. Wire

YES
NO
HOW MUCH DOES IT COST?
AVAILABLE NOW?
__ DAYS?
__ WEEKS?

2. 刹車靴

3. 化油器

4. 鏈

5. 離合器

6. 兩極眞空管

7. 驅動凸緣

8. 驅動機構

9. 驅動軸

0. 電線

1. 汽油泵浦

2. 齒輪箱

3. 螺帽鎖圈

4. 螺絲

5. 主要承接 / 傳動鏈連接套

6. 螺帽

7. 整流器

8. 發電機轉子

9. 板金螺絲

0. 線圈　伊爾

1. 起動馬達

2. 閥門

3. 墊圈

4. 車輪軸承

5. 電線

是

不是

多少錢？

現在有嗎？

____天？

____星期？

AT THE REFUELING STATION

1. Do you have 95 octane, leaded or 4-Star?
2. Super?
3. Unleaded?
4. Is this the main road to __ ?
5. Will this road go to __ ?
6. To the left
7. Straight ahead
8. To the right
9. Behind
10. Is there a motorcycle repair shop near here?
11. About how many kilometers to __ ?

PARTS & SERVICE

12. I have a dead battery. Do you have jumper cables/jump leads?
13. The Positive (+) Terminal
14. The Negative (-) Terminal
15. Can you charge my battery?
16. Can you please give me a push start/bump start?
17. Do you have distilled water?
18. Do you have a new battery?
19. Can you adjust my valves? My intake is __ , my exhaust is __ .
20. Do you have shims?
21. The engine won't start. Can you check-out the problem?
22. The engine is running rough. Can you check-out the problem?

YES
NO
HOW MUCH DOES IT COST?
AVAILABLE NOW?
__ DAYS?
__ WEEKS?

THAI
(ภาษาไทย)

TRANSLATED BY HONDA OF THAILAND

The
ENDLESS
RIDE

ที่ปั๊มน้ำมัน

1. คุณมีน้ำมันที่มีค่าอ๊อกเทน ๑๑/๙๐ หรือไม่?

2. มีน้ำมันซูเปอร์หรือไม่?

3. มีน้ำมันไร้สารตะกั่วหรือไม่?

4. ถนนสายนี้เป็นถนนหลวงไปสู่.............ใช่หรือไม่?

5. ถนนสายนี้ไป...............หรือไม่?

6. ไปทางซ้าย

7. ตรงไปข้างหน้า

8. ไปทางขวา

9. ข้างหลัง

10. มีร้านซ่อมรถจักรยานยนต์ใกล้ๆแถวนี้หรือไม่?

11. ประมาณกี่กิโลเมตร?

อะไหล่และการบริการ

12. แบตเตอรี่ไฟหมดครับ คุณมีสายพ่วงหรือเปล่า?

13. ขั้วบวก (+)

14. ขั้วลบ (−)

15. คุณชาร์จแบตเตอรี่ให้ผมหน่อยได้ไหมครับ?

16. คุณช่วยเข็นรถให้เครื่องติดให้หน่อยได้ไหมครับ?

17. มีน้ำกลั่นไหมครับ?

18. มีแบตเตอรี่ใหม่ไหมครับ?

19. ช่วยปรับวาล์วให้หน่อยได้ไหมครับ?
    ระยะห่างวาล์วไอดีของรถผม−.................. ไอเสีย−...................

20. คุณมีสกูปรับตั้งหรือชิมหรือเปล่า?

21. เครื่องยนต์ไม่ติด คุณช่วยเช็คให้หน่อยได้ไหมครับ?

22. เครื่องยนต์เดินไม่เรียบ กรุณาเช็คให้ด้วยนะครับ?

มี
ไม่มี
ราคาเท่าไหร่
มีตอนนี้ไหม?.............
วัน?.........................
อาทิตย์?.....................

23. I have an unusual sound in the engine.
Can you check-out the problem?

24. I have an unusual sound in the gear box.
Can you check-out the problem?

25. I have an unusual sound in the final drive.
Can you check-out the problem?

26. Can you service my cooling system?

27. Can you change the thermostat?

28. Can you tighten the spokes?

29. Can you service my front brakes?

30. Can you service my rear brakes?

31. Can you change the oil in my motorcycle?

32. Can you fix a puncture?

33. Do you have compressed air?

34. Do you have anti-freeze?

35. Do you have brake/clutch fluid?

36. Do you have 4-stroke engine oil?

37. Do you have 2-stroke engine oil?

38. Do you have octane booster?

39. I need a tubeless type front tire. Do you have a __ x __ x __ tire?

40. I need a tubeless type rear tire. Do you have a __ x __ x __ tire?

41. I need a tube type front tire. Do you have a __ x __ x __ tire?

42. Do you have an inner tube for this tire?

43. I need a tube type rear tire. Do you have a __ x __ x __ tire?

44. Can you change the tire?

YES
NO
HOW MUCH DOES IT COST?
AVAILABLE NOW?
__ DAYS?
__ WEEKS?

THE ENDLESS RIDE

23. เครื่องยนต์มีเสียงดังผิดปกติ ช่วยเช็คให้หน่อยได้ไหมครับ?

24. มีเสียงดังผิดปกติในห้องเกียร์ ช่วยเช็คให้หน่อยได้ไหมครับ?

25. มีเสียงดังผิดปกติในช่วงขับเคลื่อนสุดท้าย ช่วยเช็คให้ด้วยนะครับ

26. ช่วยตรวจเช็คระบบทำความเย็นให้หน่อยได้ไหมครับ?

27. ช่วยเปลี่ยนเทอร์โมสัท (เครื่องควบคุมความร้อน) ให้หน่อยได้ไหมครับ?

28. ช่วยขันซี่ลวดให้หน่อยได้ไหมครับ?

29. ช่วยตรวจดูเบรคหน้าให้หน่อยได้ไหมครับ?

30. ช่วยเช็คเบรคหลังให้หน่อยได้ไหมครับ?

31. ช่วยเปลี่ยนน้ำมันเครื่องของรถจักรยานยนต์ของผมด้วย?

32. ช่วยปะยางให้ได้ไหมครับ?

33. มีเครื่องปั๊มพ์ลมหรือเปล่าครับ?

34. มีน้ำยากันการแข็งตัวหรือไม่?

35. มีน้ำมันเบรคหรือน้ำมันคลัทช์หรือไม่?

36. คุณมีน้ำมันเครื่อง 4 ที หรือไม่?

37. คุณมีน้ำมันเครื่อง 2 ที หรือไม่?

38. มีอ๊อคเทนบูสเตอร์หรือเปล่าครับ?

39. ผมอยากได้ยางหน้าแบบไม่มียางใน
    มียางขนาด.................X................X.................หรือเปล่าครับ?

40. ผมอยากได้ยางหลังแบบไม่มียางใน
    มียางขนาด.................X................X.................ไหมครับ?

41 ผมอยากได้ยางหน้าแบบมียางในด้วย
    มียางขนาด.................X................X.................ไหมครับ?

42. มียางในสำหรับยางรุ่นนี้ไหมครับ?

43. ผมอยากได้ยางหลังแบบมียางใน
    มียางขนาด.................X................X.................ไหมครับ?

44. เปลี่ยนยางได้ไหมครับ?

มี
ไม่มี
ราคาเท่าไหร่
มีตอนนี้ไหม?.............
วัน?........................
อาทิตย์?....................

45. I need some spark plugs. Do you have this type?

46. I need an air filter. Do you have this type?

47. I need a fuel filter. Do you have this type?

48. I need an oil filter. Do you have this type?

49. Do you have a brake cable?

50. Do you have a choke cable?

51. Do you have a clutch cable?

52. Do you have a speedometer cable?

53. Do you have a throttle cable?

54. Do you have a 10 amp fuse?

55. Do you have a 15 amp fuse?

56. Do you have a main fuse?

57. Do you have starter brushes?

58. Do you have a bus or blade fuse?

59. Do you have an ACG plug?

60. Do you have a head light bulb/globe?

61. Do you have a tail light bulb/globe?

62. Do you have a turn indicator bulb/globe?

63. Do you have instrument bulbs/globes?

64. Do you have valve/rocker cover gaskets?

65. Do you have valve/rocker cover bolt packings?

66. Do you have a chain and sprocket?

67. Do you have a master link/drive chain joint?

FRAME & ENGINE WORDS

68. Alternator/generator

69. Battery

70. Bolt

YES
NO
HOW MUCH DOES IT COST?
AVAILABLE NOW?
__ DAYS?
__ WEEKS?

45. ผมอยากได้หัวเทียน มีแบบนี้ไหมครับ?

46. ผมอยากได้ไส้กรองอากาศ มีแบบนี้ไหมครับ?

47. ผมอยากได้ไส้กรองน้ำมันเชื้อเพลิง มีรุ่นนี้ไหมครับ?

48. ผมอยากได้ที่กรองน้ำมันเครื่อง มีแบบนี้ไหมครับ?

49. มีสายเบรคไหม?

50. มีสายโช้คไหม?

51. มีสายคลัทช์ไหม?

52. มีสายมาตรวัดความเร็วไหม?

53. มีสายคันเร่งมั้ย?

54. มีฟิวส์ขนาด 10 แอมป์หรือไม่?

55. มีฟิวส์ขนาด 15 แอมป์หรือไม่?

56. มีฟิวส์รวมหรือเปล่า?

57. มีเครื่องแปลงถ่านมอเตอร์สตาร์ทหรือไม่?

58. มีฟิวส์แบบ "บัส" หรือ "เบลด" หรือไม่?

59. มีปลั๊กเจนเนอเรเตอร์หรือไม่?

60. มีไฟหน้าไหม?

61. มีหลอดไฟท้ายไหม?

62. มีหลอดไฟเลี้ยวหรือไม่?

63. มีหลอดไฟสัญญาณไหม?

64. มีปะเก็นฝาครอบวาล์วหรือไม่?

65. มีโบลท์ฝาครอบวาล์วหรือไม่?

66. มีโซ่ขับเคลื่อนกับสเตอหน้าไหม?

67. มีข้อต่อไหม?

ศัพท์ตัวถังและเครื่องยนต์

68. อัลเตอร์เนเตอร์/เยนเนอเรเตอร์

69. แบตเตอรี่

70. โบลท์

มี
ไม่มี
ราคาเท่าไหร่
มีตอนนี้ไหม?..............
วัน?......................
อาทิตย์?....................

385

71. Brake pad

72. Brake shoes

73. Carburetor

74. Chain

75. Clutch

76. Diodes

77. Drive flange

78. Drive line

79. Drive shaft

80. Electrical wire

81. Fuel pump

82. Gear box

83. Lock nut

84. Machine screw

85. Master link/drive chain joint

86. Nut

87. Rectifier

88. Rotor

89. Sheet metal screw

90. Solenoid

91. Starter motor

92. Valve

93. Washer

94. Wheel bearing

95. Wire

YES
NO
HOW MUCH DOES IT COST?
AVAILABLE NOW?
__ DAYS?
__ WEEKS?

71. ผ้าดิสก์เบรค
72. ผ้าเบรค
73. คาร์บูเรเตอร์
74. โซ่ขับเคลื่อน
75. คลัทช์
76. **ไดโอ**
77. จานโซ่
78. คันส่ง
79. เพลาขับ
80. สายไฟ
81. ปั๊มน้ำมันเชื้อเพลง
82. ห้องเกียร์
83. น๊อตล๊อค
84. สกรู
85. ข้อต่อ
86. น๊อต
87. เร็คดีไฟเออร์
88. โรเตอร์
89. สกรูโลหะแผ่น
90. โซลินอยด์สตาร์ท
91. มอเตอร์สตาร์ท
92. วาล์ว วาล์ว
93. แหวนรอง
94. แบร์ริ่งล้อ
95. สายไฟ

มี
ไม่มี
ราคาเท่าไหร่
มีตอนนี้ไหม? ....
วัน? ....
อาทิตย์? ....

AT THE REFUELING STATION

1. Do you have 95 octane, leaded or 4-Star?
2. Super?
3. Unleaded?
4. Is this the main road to __ ?
5. Will this road go to __ ?
6. To the left
7. Straight ahead
8. To the right
9. Behind
10. Is there a motorcycle repair shop near here?
11. About how many kilometers to __ ?

PARTS & SERVICE

12. I have a dead battery. Do you have jumper cables/jump leads?
13. The Positive (+) Terminal
14. The Negative (-) Terminal
15. Can you charge my battery?
16. Can you please give me a push start/bump start?
17. Do you have distilled water?
18. Do you have a new battery?
19. Can you adjust my valves? My intake is __ , my exhaust is __ .
20. Do you have shims?
21. The engine won't start. Can you check-out the problem?

YES
NO
HOW MUCH DOES IT COST?
AVAILABLE NOW?
__ DAYS?
__ WEEKS?

주유소에서

1. 옥탄가가 95인 휘발유 있습니까?

2. 고급입니까?

3. 무연 휘발유입니까?

4. 이길이 _____으로 가는 길입니까?

5. 이길로 가면 _____에 갑니까?

6. 왼쪽으로

7. 곧바로 앞으로

8. 오른쪽으로

9. 뒤

10. 이 근처에 모터싸이클의 수리정이 있습니까?

11. 대략 몇 Km입니까?

부품과 서비스

12. 밧데리가 방전되었습니다. 점프 케이블이 있습니까?

13. 프러스 단자

14. 마이너스 단자

15. 밧데리를 충전시킬 수 있습니까?

16. 시동을 걸려고 하는데 뒤에서 차를 밀어 주시겠습니까?

17. 증류수 있습니까?

18. 새 밧데리가 있습니까?

19. 발브를 조정할 수 있습니까? 흡입은 ____, 배기는 ____

20. 어져스터 스큐류가 있습니까?

21. 엔진의 시동이 안걸립니다. 무엇이 잘못됐는지 봐주시겠습니까?

예

아니오

얼마입니까?

지금 있습니까?

_____일?

_____주?

22. The engine is running rough. Can you check-out the problem?

23. I have an unusual sound in the engine.
    Can you check-out the problem?

24. I have an unusual sound in the gear box.
    Can you check-out the problem?

25. I have an unusual sound in the final drive.
    Can you check-out the problem?

26. Can you service my cooling system?

27. Can you change the thermostat?

28. Can you tighten the spokes?

29. Can you service my front brakes?

30. Can you service my rear brakes?

31. Can you change the oil in my motorcycle?

32. Can you fix a puncture?

33. Do you have compressed air?

34. Do you have anti-freeze?

35. Do you have brake/clutch fluid?

36. Do you have 4-stroke engine oil?

37. Do you have 2-stroke engine oil?

38. Do you have octane booster?

39. I need a tubeless type front tire. Do you have a __ x __ x __ tire?

40. I need a tubeless type rear tire. Do you have a __ x __ x __ tire?

41. I need a tube type front tire. Do you have a __ x __ x __ tire?

42. Do you have an inner tube for this tire?

YES
NO
HOW MUCH DOES IT COST?
AVAILABLE NOW?
__ DAYS?
__ WEEKS?

22. 엔진의 상태가 좋지 않습니다. 무엇이 잘못됐는지
　　봐주시겠습니까?

23. 엔진에서 이상한 소리가 나고 있습니다. 무엇이 잘못됐는지
　　봐주시겠습니까?

24. 기아 박스에서 이상한 소리가 나고 있습니다. 무엇이 잘못됐는지
　　봐주시겠습니까?

25. 뒷바퀴에서 이상한 소리가 나고 있습니다. 무엇이 잘못됐는지
　　봐주시겠습니까?

26. 냉각계통을 수리할 수 있습니까?

27. 써모스타트를 교환할 수 있습니까?

28. 스포크를 조여줄 수 있습니까?

29. 후론트 브레이크를 수리할 수 있습니까?

30. 뒷바퀴를 수리할 수 있습니까?

31. 내 오토바이의 오일을 교환할 수 있습니까?

32. 빵꾸를 때울 수 있습니까?

33. 에어 콤프레샤가 있습니까?

34. 부동액 있습니까?

35. 브레이크나 크럿치액이 있습니까?

36. 4 싸이클 엔진 오일 있습니까?

37. 2 싸이클 엔진 오일 있습니까?

38. 휘발유 첨가제 있습니까?

39. 튜브레스로 된 앞 타이어가 필요합니다. ＿＿＿＿＿ 타이어
　　있습니까?

40. 튜브레스로 된 뒷 타이어가 필요합니다. ＿＿＿＿＿ 타이어
　　있습니까?

41. 튜브레스로 된 앞 타이어가 필요합니다. ＿＿＿＿＿ 타이어
　　있습니까?

42. 이 타이어에 맞는 쥬브 있습니다?

예

아니오

얼마입니까?

지금 있습니까?

＿＿＿＿일?

＿＿＿＿주?

43. I need a tube type rear tire. Do you have a __ x __ x __ tire?

44. Can you change the tire?

45. I need some spark plugs. Do you have this type?

46. I need an air filter. Do you have this type?

47. I need a fuel filter. Do you have this type?

48. I need an oil filter. Do you have this type?

49. Do you have a brake cable?

50. Do you have a choke cable?

51. Do you have a clutch cable?

52. Do you have a speedometer cable?

53. Do you have a throttle cable?

54. Do you have a 10 amp fuse?

55. Do you have a 15 amp fuse?

56. Do you have a main fuse?

57. Do you have starter brushes?

58. Do you have a bus or blade fuse?

59. Do you have an ACG plug?

60. Do you have a head light bulb/globe?

61. Do you have a tail light bulb/globe?

62. Do you have a turn indicator bulb/globe?

63. Do you have instrument bulbs/globes?

64. Do you have valve/rocker cover gaskets?

65. Do you have valve/rocker cover bolt packings?

66. Do you have a chain and sprocket?

67. Do you have a master link/drive chain joint?

YES
NO
HOW MUCH DOES IT COST?
AVAILABLE NOW?
__ DAYS?
__ WEEKS?

43. 튜브레스로 된 타이어가 필요합니다. _____ 타이어 있습니까?
44. 타이어 교환을 할 수 있습니까?
45. 스파크 프러그가 필요합니다. 이런 타입의 프러그가 있습니다?
46. 공기 휠타가 필요합니다. 이런 타입으로 있습니까?
47. 연료 휠타가 필요합니다. 이런 타입으로 있습니까?
48. 오일 휠타가 필요합니다. 이런 타입으로 있습니까?
49. 브레이크 케이블 있습니까?
50. 쵸크 케이블 있습니까?
51. 크럿치 케이블 있습니까?
52. 스피드 메타 케이블 있습니까?
53. 쓰로틀 케이블 있습니까?
54. 10 암페아짜리 휴즈 있습니까?
55. 15 암페아짜리 휴즈 있습니까?
56. 메인 휴즈 있습니까?
57. 스타트 모터의 브러쉬 있습니까?
58. 프라스틱 타입의 휴즈 있습니까?
59. AC 제네레이타 프러그 있습니까?
60. 헤드라이트 있습니까?
61. 테일라이트 전구 있습니까?
62. 윙카 전구 있습니까?
63. 메타판의 전구 있습니까?
64. 헤드카바 가스켓트 있습니까?
65. 헤드카바 볼트의 바킹 있습니까?
66. 체인과 스프로켓 있습니까?
67. 체인의 크립 있습니까?

예
아니오
얼마입니까?
지금 있습니까?
_____일?
_____주?

FRAME & ENGINE WORDS

68. Alternator/generator
69. Battery
70. Bolt
71. Brake pad
72. Brake shoes
73. Carburetor
74. Chain
75. Clutch
76. Diodes
77. Drive flange
78. Drive line
79. Drive shaft
80. Electrical wire
81. Fuel pump
82. Gear box
83. Lock nut
84. Machine screw
85. Master link/drive chain joint
86. Nut
87. Rectifier
88. Rotor
89. Sheet metal screw
90. Solenoid
91. Starter motor
92. Valve
93. Washer
94. Wheel bearing
95. Wire

YES
NO
HOW MUCH DOES IT COST?
AVAILABLE NOW?
__ DAYS?
__ WEEKS?

8. 알터네이터 / 제네레이타
9. 밧데리
0. 볼트
1. 브레이크 패드
2. 브레이크 슈
3. 캬브레이타
4. 체인
5. 크럿치
6. 다이오드
7. 드라이브 후렌지
8. 구동 계통
9. 드라이브 샤프트
0. 배선
1. 휴일 펌프
2. 기어 박스
3. 로크 넛트
4. 머신 스쿠류
5. 조인트 렁크
6. 넛트
7. 렉티화이어
8. 로타
9. 관음용 스쿠류
0. 솔레노이드
1. 스타터 모타
2. 밸브 밸브
3. 와샤
4. 휠 베아링
5. 와이어

예
아니오
얼마입니까 ?
지금 있습니까 ?
_____일 ?

AT THE REFUELING STATION

1. Do you have 95 octane, leaded or 4-Star?
2. Super?
3. Unleaded?
4. Is this the main road to __ ?
5. Will this road go to __ ?
6. To the left
7. Straight ahead
8. To the right
9. Behind
10. Is there a motorcycle repair shop near here?
11. About how many kilometers to __ ?

PARTS & SERVICE

12. I have a dead battery. Do you have jumper cables/jump leads?
13. The Positive (+) Terminal
14. The Negative (-) Terminal
15. Can you charge my battery?
16. Can you please give me a push start/bump start?
17. Do you have distilled water?
18. Do you have a new battery?
19. Can you adjust my valves? My intake is __ , my exhaust is __ .
20. Do you have shims?
21. The engine won't start. Can you check-out the problem?
22. The engine is running rough. Can you check-out the problem?
23. I have an unusual sound in the engine.
    Can you check-out the problem?

YES
NO
HOW MUCH DOES IT COST?
AVAILABLE NOW?
__ DAYS?
__ WEEKS?

JAPANESE
（日本語）

TRANSLATED BY HONDA OF JAPAN

The
ENDLESS
RIDE

ガソリン・スタンドにて

1. 95オクタンのガソリンはありますか？

2. スーパー（ハイオクタン）ですか？

3. 無鉛ですか？

4. これは＿＿＿へ行くメイン道路ですか？

5. この道は＿＿＿へ行きますか？

6. 左へ。

7. 真っ直ぐ前。

8. 右へ。

9. 後ろ。

10. オートバイの修理所が近くにありますか？

11. ＿＿＿までおよそ何キロぐらいですか？

部品とサービス

12. バッテリーがだめです。バッテリーコードを持っていますか？

13. プラスのターミナル。

14. マイナスのターミナル。

15. 私のバッテリーを充電してくれますか？

16. 押しがけしてもらえますか？

17. 蒸留水を持っていますか？

18. 新しいバッテリーを持っていますか？

19. バルブを調節してくれますか？ 吸入は＿＿＿、排気は＿＿＿です。

20. シムを持っていますか？

21. エンジンがかからないのですが、原因をチェックしてもらえますか？

22. エンジンの調子がよくありません。原因をチェックしてもらえ
　　ますか？

23. エンジンから変な音がするので原因をチェックしてもらえますか？

はい

いいえ

いくらですか？

現在、ありますか？

＿＿＿日？

＿＿＿週？

397

24. I have an unusual sound in the gear box.
Can you check-out the problem?

25. I have an unusual sound in the final drive.
Can you check-out the problem?

26. Can you service my cooling system?

27. Can you change the thermostat?

28. Can you tighten the spokes?

29. Can you service my front brakes?

30. Can you service my rear brakes?

31. Can you change the oil in my motorcycle?

32. Can you fix a puncture?

33. Do you have compressed air?

34. Do you have anti-freeze?

35. Do you have brake/clutch fluid?

36. Do you have 4-stroke engine oil?

37. Do you have 2-stroke engine oil?

38. Do you have octane booster?

39. I need a tubeless type front tire. Do you have a __ x __ x __ tire?

40. I need a tubeless type rear tire. Do you have a __ x __ x __ tire?

41. I need a tube type front tire. Do you have a __ x __ x __ tire?

42. Do you have an inner tube for this tire?

43. I need a tube type rear tire. Do you have a __ x __ x __ tire?

44. Can you change the tire?

45. I need some spark plugs. Do you have this type?

46. I need an air filter. Do you have this type?

47. I need a fuel filter. Do you have this type?

48. I need an oil filter. Do you have this type?

49. Do you have a brake cable?

YES
NO
HOW MUCH DOES IT COST?
AVAILABLE NOW?
__ DAYS?
__ WEEKS?

24. ギヤボックスから変な音がするので原因をチェックしてもらえますか？

25. デフから変な音がするので原因をチェックしてもらえますか？

26. 冷却装置をみてくれますか？

27. サーモスタットを交換してくれますか？

28. スポークをきつく締めてくれますか？

29. フロントブレーキをみてくれますか？

30. リアブレーキをみてくれますか？

31. 私のオートバイのオイルを交換してくれますか？

32. パンクの修理をしてくれますか？

33. 圧縮空気をあつかっていますか？

34. 不凍液はありますか？

35. ブレーキ液（クラッチ液）はありますか？

36. 4 ストロークのエンジン・オイルはありますか？

37. 2 ストロークのエンジン・オイルはありますか？

38. オクタン価を上げるガソリン添加物がありますか？

39. チューブレスの前輪タイヤが必要です。＿＿ × ＿＿ × ＿＿のタイヤはありますか？

40. チューブレスの後輪タイヤが必要です。＿＿ × ＿＿ × ＿＿のタイヤはありますか？

41. チューブ入りの前輪タイヤが必要です。＿＿ × ＿＿ × ＿＿のタイヤはありますか？

42. このタイヤのインナ・チューブがありますか？

43. チューブ入りの後輪タイヤが必要です。＿＿ × ＿＿ × ＿＿のタイヤはありますか？

44. タイヤ交換してくれますか？

45. スパークプラグが必要です。このタイプはありますか？

46. エアーフィルターが必要です。このタイプはありますか？

47. フュエル・フィルターが必要です。このタイプはありますか？

48. オイルフィルターが必要です。このタイプはありますか？

49. ブレーキのワイヤーはありますか？

はい

いいえ

いくらですか？

現在、ありますか？

＿＿日？

＿＿週？

50. Do you have a choke cable?

51. Do you have a clutch cable?

52. Do you have a speedometer cable?

53. Do you have a throttle cable?

54. Do you have a 10 amp fuse?

55. Do you have a 15 amp fuse?

56. Do you have a main fuse?

57. Do you have starter brushes?

58. Do you have a bus or blade fuse?

59. Do you have an ACG plug?

60. Do you have a head light bulb/globe?

61. Do you have a tail light bulb/globe?

62. Do you have a turn indicator bulb/globe?

63. Do you have instrument bulbs/globes?

64. Do you have valve/rocker cover gaskets?

65. Do you have valve/rocker cover bolt packings?

66. Do you have a chain and sprocket?

67. Do you have a master link/drive chain joint?

FRAME & ENGINE WORDS

68. Alternator/generator

69. Battery

70. Bolt

71. Brake pad

72. Brake shoes

73. Carburetor

74. Chain

75. Clutch

YES
NO
HOW MUCH DOES IT COST?
AVAILABLE NOW?
__ DAYS?
__ WEEKS?

50. チョークのワイヤーはありますか？

51. クラッチのワイヤーはありますか？

52. スピートメーターのワイヤーはありますか？

53. スロットル（アクセル）のワイヤーはありますか？

54. 10アンペアのヒューズはありますか？

55. 15アンペアのヒューズはありますか？

56. メインヒューズはありますか？

57. スターター（セルモータ）のブラシはありますか？

58. バス（ガラスのタイプ）かブレイド（プラスチック）のヒューズは
　　ありますか？

59. ACGプラグはありますか？

60. ヘッドライトの電球はありますか？

61. テールライトの電球はありますか？

62. 方向指示器（ウインカー）の電球はありますか？

63. 計器（メーター）の電球はありますか？

64. バルブカバー（ヘッドカバー）のガスケットはありますか？

65. バルブカバー（ヘッドカバー）のボルトパッキングはありますか？

66. チェーンとスプロケットはありますか？

67. マスターリンク（チェーンのジョイント）はありますか？

フレーム及びエンジン用語

68. オルタネータ（発電器）

69. バッテリー

70. ボルト

71. ブレーキパッド

72. ブレーキシュー

73. キャブレター

74. チェーン

75. クラッチ

はい

いいえ

いくらですか？

現在、ありますか？

＿＿＿日？

＿＿＿週？

76. Diodes

77. Drive flange

78. Drive line

79. Drive shaft

80. Electrical wire

81. Fuel pump

82. Gear box

83. Lock nut

84. Machine screw

85. Master link/drive chain joint

86. Nut

87. Rectifier

88. Rotor

89. Sheet metal screw

90. Solenoid

91. Starter motor

92. Valve

93. Washer

94. Wheel bearing

95. Wire

YES
NO
HOW MUCH DOES IT COST?
AVAILABLE NOW?
__ DAYS?
__ WEEKS?

76. ダイオード
77. ドライブフランジ（後ろのドライブシャフトのカバー）
78. ドライブ・ライン（駆動系）
79. ドライブシャフト
80. 電気ワイヤー（配線）
81. 燃料ポンプ
82. ギヤボックス
83. ロックナット
84. 機械用ネジ
85. マスターリンク（チェーンジョイント）
86. ナット
87. 整流器
88. ローター
89. シートメタル ネジ
90. ソレノイド
91. スターターモーター（セルモーター）
92. バルブ
93. ワッシャー
94. 車輪ベアリング
95. ワイヤー

はい
いいえ
いくらですか？
現在、ありますか？
＿＿＿日？
＿＿＿週？

AT THE REFUELING STATION

1. Do you have 95 octane, leaded or 4-Star?

2. Super?

3. Unleaded?

4. Is this the main road to __ ?

5. Will this road go to __ ?

6. To the left

7. Straight ahead

8. To the right

9. Behind

10. Is there a motorcycle repair shop near here?

11. About how many kilometers to __ ?

PARTS & SERVICE

12. I have a dead battery. Do you have jumper cables/jump leads?

13. The Positive (+) Terminal

14. The Negative (-) Terminal

15. Can you charge my battery?

16. Can you please give me a push start/bump start?

17. Do you have distilled water?

18. Do you have a new battery?

19. Can you adjust my valves? My intake is __ , my exhaust is __ .

20. Do you have shims?

21. The engine won't start. Can you check-out the problem?

22. The engine is running rough. Can you check-out the problem?

23. I have an unusual sound in the engine.
    Can you check-out the problem?

YES
NO
HOW MUCH DOES IT COST?
AVAILABLE NOW?
__ DAYS?
__ WEEKS?

TRANSLATED BY HONDA OF MEXICO/SPAIN

MEXICAN/SPANISH
(MEXICANO/ESPAÑOL)

The
ENDLESS
RIDE

EN LA ESTACIÓN DE GASOLINA

1. ¿Tiene 95 octano?
2. ¿Super?
3. ¿MAGNA SIN?
4. ¿Es esté el camino principal a __ ?
5. ¿Irá este camino a __ ?
6. A la izquierda
7. Derecho
8. A la derecha
9. Atrás
10. ¿Habrá un taller de reparación de motocicleta cerca de aquí?
11. ¿Sobre cuántos kilometros?

REFACCIONES Y SERVICIO DE REPARACIÓN

12. Tengo una batería descargada. ¿Tiene cables de pasa corriente?
13. El Terminal (+) Positivo
14. El Terminal (-) Negativo
15. ¿Puede cargarme la batería?
16. ¿Puede empujarme?
17. ¿Tiene agua distilada?
18. ¿Tiene una batería nueva?
19. ¿Puede ajustar las válvulas?
    Mi holgura en admision es __ , y mi escape es __ .
20. ¿Tiene el eje oscilante/calzas?
21. El motor no arranca. ¿Puede inspeccionar el problema?
22. El motor esta corriendo agitado. ¿Puede inspeccionar el problema?
23. Hay un sonido raro en el motor. ¿Puede inspeccionar el problema?

SÍ
NO
¿CUANTO ES?
¿DISPONIBLE AHORA?
¿__ DÍAS?
¿__SEMANAS?

405

24. I have an unusual sound in the gear box.
Can you check-out the problem?

25. I have an unusual sound in the final drive.
Can you check-out the problem?

26. Can you service my cooling system?

27. Can you change the thermostat?

28. Can you tighten the spokes?

29. Can you service my front brakes?

30. Can you service my rear brakes?

31. Can you change the oil in my motorcycle?

32. Can you fix a puncture?

33. Do you have compressed air?

34. Do you have anti-freeze?

35. Do you have brake/clutch fluid?

36. Do you have 4-stroke engine oil?

37. Do you have 2-stroke engine oil?

38. Do you have octane booster?

39. I need a tubeless type front tire.
Do you have a __ x __ x __ tire?

40. I need a tubeless type rear tire.
Do you have a __ x __ x __ tire?

41. I need a tube type front tire.
Do you have a __ x __ x __ tire?

42. Do you have an inner tube for this tire?

43. I need a tube type rear tire.
Do you have a __ x __ x __ tire?

44. Can you change the tire?

45. I need some spark plugs. Do you have this type?

46. I need an air filter. Do you have this type?

YES
NO
HOW MUCH DOES IT COST?
AVAILABLE NOW?
__ DAYS?
__ WEEKS?

406

MEXICAN/SPANISH
(MEXICANO/ESPAÑOL)

TRANSLATED BY HONDA OF MEXICO/SPAIN

The
ENDLESS
RIDE

24. Hay un sonido raro en la caja de cambio.
    ¿Puede inspeccionar el problema?

25. Hay un sonido raro en la transmisión.
    ¿Puede inspeccionar el problema?

26. ¿Puede cambiarme el agua del radiador?

27. ¿Puede cambiarme el termóstato?

28. ¿Puede ajustar los rayos de las llantas?

29. ¿Puede reparar los frenos delanteros?

30. ¿Puede reparar los frenos traseros?

31. ¿Puede cambiar el aceite en mi motocicleta?

32. ¿Puede arreglar el pinchazo en la neumático/llanta?

33. ¿Tiene aire a presión?

34. ¿Tiene anti-congelante?

35. ¿Tiene liquido de freno/embrague?

36. ¿Tiene aceite de motor cuatro tiempos?

37. ¿Tiene aceite de motor dos tiempos?

38. ¿Tiene aditivos para aumentare el poder de la gasolina/octano?

39. Necesito una llanta delantera sin cámara/tubo interior.
    ¿Tiene tamaño a __ x __ x __ de neumático/llanta?

40. Necesito una llanta trasera sin cámara/tubo interior.
    ¿Tiene tamaño a __ x __ x __ de neumático/llanta?

41. Necesito una llanta delantera con cámara/tubo interior.
    ¿Tiene tamaño a __ x __ x __ neumático/llanta?

42. ¿Tiene una cámara/tubo para esta neumático/llanta?

43. Necesito una llanta trasera con cámara interior.
    ¿Tiene tamaño a __ x __ x __ de neumático/llanta?

44. ¿Puede cambiar el neumático/ la llanta?

45. Necesito unas bujías. ¿Tiene este tipo?

46. Necesito un filtro de aire. ¿Tiene de este tipo?

SÍ
NO
¿CUANTO ES?
¿DISPONIBLE AHORA?
¿__ DÍAS?
¿__SEMANAS?

47. I need a fuel filter. Do you have this type?

48. I need an oil filter. Do you have this type?

49. Do you have a brake cable?

50. Do you have a choke cable?

51. Do you have a clutch cable?

52. Do you have a speedometer cable?

53. Do you have a throttle cable?

54. Do you have a 10 amp fuse?

55. Do you have a 15 amp fuse?

56. Do you have a main fuse?

57. Do you have starter brushes?

58. Do you have a bus or blade fuse?

59. Do you have an ACG plug?

60. Do you have a head light bulb/globe?

61. Do you have a tail light bulb/globe?

62. Do you have a turn indicator bulb/globe?

63. Do you have instrument bulbs/globes?

64. Do you have valve/rocker cover gaskets?

65. Do you have valve/rocker cover bolt packings?

66. Do you have a chain and sprocket?

67. Do you have a master link/drive chain joint?

FRAME & ENGINE WORDS

68. Alternator/generator

69. Battery

70. Bolt

71. Brake pad

72. Brake shoes

YES
NO
HOW MUCH DOES IT COST?
AVAILABLE NOW?
__ DAYS?
__ WEEKS?

MEXICAN/SPANISH
(MEXICANO/ESPAÑOL)

TRANSLATED BY HONDA OF MEXICO/SPAIN

The
ENDLESS
RIDE

47. Necesito un filtro de combustible. ¿Tiene uno de este tipo?

48. Necesito un filtro de aceite. ¿Tiene uno de este tipo?

49. ¿Tiene un cable de frenos?

50. ¿Tiene un cable regulador de aire/choke?

51. ¿Tiene un cable de embrague?

52. ¿Tiene un cable de velocímetro?

53. ¿Tiene un cable de acelerador/regulador?

54. ¿Tiene un fusible de 10 amp (ampere)?

55. ¿Tiene un fusible de 15 amp (ampere)?

56. ¿Tiene un fusible principal?

57. ¿Tiene escobillas de arranque?

58. ¿Tiene un fusible de barra común o uno de álabe?

59. ¿Tiene una bujía de ACG?

60. ¿Tiene faro/foco delantero?

61. ¿Tiene una bombilla/foco piloto?

62. ¿Tiene una bombilla/foco para el intermitente?

63. ¿Tiene bombillas/focos para el tablero?

64. ¿Tiene retenes/empaques con válvulas forradas/tapaderas?

65. ¿Tiene retenes/empaques de pernos con válvulas forradas/tapaderas?

66. ¿Tiene una cadena y piñon/engrane?

67. ¿Tiene el eslabón principal?

BASTIDOR & MOTOR PALABRAS

68. Alternador/generador

69. Batería

70. Tornillo

71. Pastilla de freno

72. Zapata de freno

SÍ
NO
¿CUANTO ES?
¿DISPONIBLE AHORA?
¿__ DÍAS?
¿__SEMANAS?

73. Carburetor

74. Chain

75. Clutch

76. Diodes

77. Drive flange

78. Drive line

79. Drive shaft

80. Electrical wire

81. Fuel pump

82. Gear box

83. Lock nut

84. Machine screw

85. Master link/drive chain joint

86. Nut

87. Rectifier

88. Rotor

89. Sheet metal screw

90. Solenoid

91. Starter motor

92. Valve

93. Washer

94. Wheel bearing

95. Wire

YES
NO
HOW MUCH DOES IT COST?
AVAILABLE NOW?
__ DAYS?
__ WEEKS?

MEXICAN/SPANISH
(MEXICANO/ESPAÑOL)

TRANSLATED BY HONDA OF MEXICO/SPAIN

The
ENDLESS
RIDE

73. Carburador
74. Cadena
75. Embrague
76. Diodos
77. Pestaña impulsor
78. -
79. Eje transmisor
80. Cableado/cable eléctrico
81. Bomba de gasolina
82. Caja de cambio
83. Contratuerca
84. Tornillo para metales
85. Eslabón principal
86. Tornillo
87. Rectificador/regulador de corriente
88. Rotor
89. Tornillo pasa fondos/pija
90. Solenoide
91. Motor de arranque/marcha
92. Válvula
93. Arandela/rondana
94. Cojinete de rueda/llanta. Valero de rueda/llanta
95. Cableado/cable

*SÍ
NO
¿CUANTO ES?
¿DISPONIBLE AHORA?
¿__ DÍAS?
¿__SEMANAS?*

24 Hour Average Monthly Riding Temperatures

City (Celsius/Fahrenheit)	Jan	Feb	Mar	April
Acapulco	24/75	24/75	26/78	27/80
Adelaide	24/75	23/73	21/69	19/66
Anchorage	-11/12	-7/19	-4/24	1/33
Amsterdam	3/37	3/37	5/41	9/48
Athens	9/48	10/50	12/53	15/59
Auckland	20/68	20/68	19/66	16/60
Bangkok	26/78	27/80	29/84	30/86
Berlin	0/32	0/32	4/39	9/48
Bombay	24/75	24/75	26/78	28/82
Brisbane	28/82	25/77	24/75	21/69
Brussels	2/35	3/37	6/42	8/46
Cairo	13/55	14/57	17/62	21/69
Calcutta	20/68	21/69	21/69	29/84
Christchurch	18/64	17/62	15/59	11/51
Copenhagen	0/32	0/32	2/35	7/44
Darwin	28/82	28/82	28/82	28/82
Delhi	14/57	15/59	20/68	29/84
Fairbanks	-23/-9	-19/-2	-12/10	-1/30
Denpasar	27/80	27/80	27/80	27/80
Frankfurt	1/33	3/37	6/42	10/50
Grand Canyon/Monument Valley	1/33	3/37	7/44	12/53
Hong Kong	15/59	15/59	18/64	22/71
Istanbul	5/41	5/41	7/44	12/53

May	June	July	Aug	Sep	Oct	Nov	Dec
29/84	30/86	30/86	30/86	28/82	28/82	27/80	28/82
15/59	12/53	11/51	12/53	14/57	17/62	19/66	22/71
8/46	12/53	14/57	13/55	9/48	1/33	-6/21	-1/30
14/57	15/59	17/62	18/64	16/60	11/51	7/44	4/39
20/68	25/77	27/80	27/80	24/75	20/68	15/59	11/51
14/57	12/53	11/51	11/51	13/55	14/57	15/59	18/64
30/86	29/84	28/82	28/82	28/82	27/80	27/80	27/80
14/57	17/62	18/64	17/62	14/57	9/48	4/39	1/33
30/86	29/84	27/80	27/80	26/78	28/82	27/80	26/78
18/64	16/60	15/59	16/60	21/69	23/73	23/73	25/77
13/55	16/60	18/64	17/62	14/57	10/50	5/41	3/37
25/77	27/80	28/82	28/82	26/78	24/75	20/68	15/59
30/86	31/87	31/87	31/87	30/86	26/78	24/75	20/68
7/44	5/41	5/41	5/41	7/44	9/48	12/53	16/60
12/53	15/59	18/64	17/62	13/55	9/48	4/39	1/33
27/80	25/77	25/77	26/78	28/82	29/84	29/84	29/84
30/86	30/86	31/87	31/87	30/86	26/78	24/75	20/68
8/46	15/59	16/60	13/55	7/44	-3/26	-16/3	-22/-7
28/82	28/82	28/82	27/80	27/80	27/80	27/80	26/78
14/57	18/64	16/60	18/64	15/59	9/48	5/41	2/35
16/60	22/71	25/77	24/75	21/69	12/53	11/51	1/33
25/77	27/80	29/84	29/84	27/80	25/77	21/69	18/64
17/62	21/69	24/75	24/75	20/68	16/60	12/53	8/46

City (Celsius/Fahrenheit)	Jan	Feb	Mar	April
Kathmandu	10/50	12/53	16/60	19/66
Kuala Lumpur	27/80	28/82	28/82	28/82
London	5/41	5/41	7/44	9/48
Los Angeles	13/55	14/57	15/59	16/60
Madras	29/84	31/87	33/91	35/95
Madrid	4/39	6/42	9/48	12/53
Manchester	4/39	4/39	5/41	8/46
Melbourne	20/68	20/68	19/66	16/60
Mexico City	12/53	14/57	16/60	18/64
Osaka	3/37	4/39	7/44	13/55
Paris	3/37	4/39	7/44	11/51
Penang	27/80	28/82	28/82	28/82
Perth	23/73	23/73	21/69	19/66
Rome	8/46	9/48	11/51	14/57
San Diego	13/55	14/57	14/57	16/60
San Francisco	10/50	12/53	13/55	13/55
Seoul	-4/24	0/32	3/37	13/55
Singapore	27/80	27/80	27/80	27/80
Sydney	22/71	22/71	21/69	19/66
Tokyo	3/37	4/39	7/44	13/55
Vancouver	3/37	5/41	6/42	9/48
Vienna	1/33	1/33	6/42	12/53
Zurich	0/32	2/35	6/42	9/48

May	June	July	Aug	Sep	Oct	Nov	Dec
22/71	24/75	24/75	24/75	23/73	20/68	15/59	11/51
28/82	27/80	27/80	28/82	28/82	27/80	27/80	27/80
12/53	16/60	18/64	17/62	15/59	11/51	7/44	5/41
18/64	20/68	22/71	22/71	22/71	20/68	17/62	14/57
33/91	37/98	35/95	35/95	34/93	32/89	29/84	29/84
16/60	21/69	24/75	23/73	19/66	14/57	8/46	6/42
9/48	13/55	16/60	15/59	13/55	10/50	6/42	4/39
3/37	11/51	10/50	11/51	13/55	15/59	16/60	18/64
19/66	19/66	19/66	18/64	17/62	15/59	14/57	12/53
17/62	21/69	25/77	26/78	23/73	17/62	11/51	6/42
13/55	17/62	19/66	18/64	16/60	11/51	6/42	4/39
28/82	28/82	28/82	27/80	27/80	27/80	27/80	27/80
16/60	14/57	13/55	13/55	14/57	16/60	19/66	21/69
18/64	22/71	25/77	25/77	22/71	18/64	13/55	9/48
17/62	19/66	21/69	22/71	21/69	19/66	16/60	14/57
15/59	15/59	15/59	15/59	16/60	16/60	14/57	8/46
15/59	20/68	24/75	25/77	20/68	13/55	7/44	0/32
28/82	28/82	28/82	28/82	28/82	27/80	27/80	27/80
15/59	13/55	12/53	13/55	15/59	18/64	20/68	21/69
17/62	21/69	25/77	26/78	23/73	17/62	11/51	6/42
12/53	15/59	17/62	17/62	14/57	10/50	6/42	4/39
15/59	19/66	21/69	20/68	17/62	11/51	6/42	1/33
14/57	17/62	19/66	19/66	16/60	10/50	5/41	1/33

Honda Worldwide Emergency Service Directory

Have an unusual problem? Need fast, friendly service? The following Honda distributors around the world can help you in the case of an emergency. Remember, your Honda After Sales Service is as close as your nearest telephone.

Europe	*City*	*Telephone*
Andorra	Andorra-La-Vella	21295
Austria	Vienna	0222/610610
Belgium	Aalst	053/760211
Czech Republic	Prague	42-2-267633
England	London	081-747-1400
France	Marne-La-Valle (Paris)	(1) 60059012
Germany	Offenbach/Main (Frankfurt)	069-83091
Gibraltar	Devil's Tower Road	79004
Greece	Athens	(01) 3458111, (01) 3467011
Ireland	Dublin	782-888
Italy	Rome	06547941
The Netherlands	Am Ridderkerk	0/1804.57333
Portugal	Sacaven (Lisbon)	(01) 9470635
Spain	Cornella (Barcelona)	93-3771000
Switzerland	Vernier-Geneve	(002) 412200
Serbia	Sr Slovenija	(061) 317033
Scandinavia		
Denmark	Arhus	(06) 174100
Finland	Vantaa (Helsinki)	089100
Norway	Ski (Oslo)	09-945000
Sweden	Kungsbacka (Goteborg)	30 014080

North Africa	City	Telephone
Morocco	Casablanca	367840, 367115, 391455

Middle East		
Iran	Teheran	820031-34

India - Pakistan		
India	New Delhi	6872451
Pakistan	Karachi	294307-8

Southeast Asia		
Malaysia	Georgetown On Penang Island	636314
Singapore	Singapore	3399002
Thailand	Bangkok	252-5432

South Asia		
Indonesia	Jakarta	490/492072492360

Australia		
Australia	Campbellfield (Melbourne)	(03) 270-1111

The Far East		
Japan	Tokyo	(03) 423-1111
South Korea	Seoul	267-6111-9

North America		
Canada	Toronto	N/A
United States	Torrance, California	N/A
Mexico	Guadalajara	688-01-01

Central America		
Costa Rica	San Jose	223350, 211122
El Salvador	San Salvador	20283
Guatemala	Guatemala City	45232, 45238
Honduras	Tegucigalpa	22-0708-9
Nicaragua	Managua	61397
Panama	Panama	23-8411

South America	City	Telephone
Argentina	Buenos Aires	766-0846, 766-1945, 766-3094
Bolivia	La Paz	354425, 354445
Brazil	Sao Paulo	572-0022, 572-0533
Chile	Santiago	74297
Columbia	Cali	64-5009
Ecuador	Cuenca	800111
French Guiana	Cayenne	722
Paraguay	Asuncion	280185-87
Peru	Lima	414141, 414172
Surinam	Paramaribo	71313
Uruguay	Montevideo	411113
Venezuela	Caracas	041-333609, 041-336514

N/A = Not Available

The Carnet de Passages

What is it?

Prior to the creation of the European Common Market, riders were required to use a Carnet de Passages whenever they crossed a European border. This carnet was an easy means of insuring that the owner would not sell his or her motorcycle without paying the duty. A carnet today is no longer needed in Europe but there are still areas of the world that require a carnet for the temporary importation of a motorcycle.

Who needs it?

Any rider planning a trip to Egypt, Jordan, Syria, Nepal, India, Pakistan, New Zealand, Australia, Africa, the Far East, South America, Singapore, etc. will need a current Carnet de Passages.

How do you get it?

The easiest way to obtain a carnet is to contact your local Automobile Association or Touring Club. If you are visiting England, contact the RAC in South Croydon (London).

To receive a carnet, three requirements must be met:

1. There is usually a club or membership fee.
2. There is a fee for the Carnet booklet itself.
3. And finally, there is the financial deposit.

What does it cost?

The yearly membership in the RAC is in the area of £70 ($100). A Carnet booklet with 10 pages, good for visiting 10 countries, costs £55 ($80). A Carnet booklet with 25 pages, good for visiting 25 countries, costs £65 ($95). Carnet booklets are valid for one year from the date of issue.

The financial deposit will depend upon the type of carnet issued (AIT, ATA, TIR) and the cost of your motorcycle. When I visited Egypt, Jordan, Syria, Malaysia and Australia, I had to deposit $8,000 with the RAC in London. Later, when I rode to India, Nepal and Singapore, my deposit was increased to $14,800.

Upon the completion of your ride, be sure to have the carnet stamped by your local customs official verifying that your motorcycle has returned to its "home country." Then return your carnet to the issuer for a refund.

Metric Conversion Tables

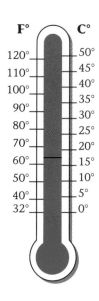

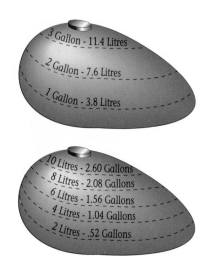

Temperature
Fahrenheit to Celsius: Subtract 32, multiply by 5 and divide by 9.
Celsius to Fahrenheit: Multiply by 9, divide by 5 and add 32.

Volume
Gallons to liters: Multiply by 3.79.
Imperial gallons to liters: Multiply by 4.55.
Liters to gallons: Multiply by 0.26.
Liters to Imperial gallons: Multiply by 0.22.

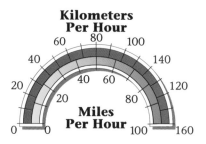

Speed Per Hour
Miles to kilometers: Multiply by 1.6.
Kilometers to miles: Multiply by .6.

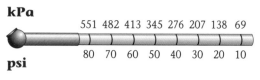

Air Pressure
Kilopascals (kPa) to Pounds per square inch (psi): Multiply by .145.
Pounds per square inch (psi) to Kilopascals (kPa): Multiply by 6.89.

The Honda Magna 700

Was it the right motorcycle to take around the world?

Since returning to the USA, I've been asked, "If you were to make this ride again, would you still chose the Honda Magna 700?"

First, I'd like to say that a rider will make a trip of this magnitude only once in a lifetime.

Second, I could have chosen a simpler, less costly, easier to maintain motorcycle, but would I have had as much fun? It would be akin to choosing between taking a 2-wheeled Volkswagen and a 2-wheeled Ferrari. Without a question, the Honda Magna 700, a high performance machine, cost more to maintain, but it was one hell of a performer! So how can you place a price on fun and adventure?

My own personal reasons for selecting the red Honda Magna 700 ranged from the logical to the bizarre.

Logical. Prior to this purchase, I had owned five other Honda motorcycles, and as I always had excellent luck with them, why change brands?

Bizarre. Believe it or not, I chose the Honda Magna 700 because of its color. That's right, its color! I knew that candy glory red would contrast well in blue – green zones like Southeast Asia, Alaska, Scandinavia, and Yucatán. And, as the basic purpose for my trip was not to ride a motorcycle around the world, but rather to *photograph* one being ridden around the world, color was of primary consideration. The radiator, the maintenance free drive shaft, the four cylinders, all of these items were great .... but they were just frosting on the cake!

So to answer the question, "Would I still chose a Honda Magna 700?"

You bet I would .... provided it was painted candy glory red!

What's Your Beer I.Q.?

Scenario: It's been a long, hot day and you have been riding for hours. But now it's over and it's time to unwind and relax. After shutting down the engine and taking off your jacket, you're served an ice-cold can of Foster's Beer.

Question: In what country have you been riding?

Now, that was easy. From here on, it gets more difficult. Match the following Brands with their Country of Origin. For the answers, hold the next page up to your rear view mirror.

Brand Name
1. VB
2. Tiger
3. Anchor
4. Singha
5. Bintang
6. Cruzcampo
7. Guinness
8. Corona
9. Budweiser
10. Labatt
11. Sagres
12. Nastro Azzuro
13. 1664
14. Stella Artois

Country Of Origin
A. Finland
B. Isle Of Man
C. Australia
D. Syria
E. Mexico
F. South Korea
G. Holland
H. Philippines
I. Sweden
J. Norway
K. Thailand
L. Spain
M. Luxembourg
N. Cyprus

Brand Name

15. Heineken
16. Carlsberg
17. Pripps
18. Beck's
19. Gosser
20. Gurten
21. Stork
22. Bushy's
23. BBBB
24. Stella
25. Goldhorn Club
26. Lapin Kulta
27. Efes Pilsen
28. Barada
29. Goldstar
30. Bullet
31. Iceberg
32. Kirin
33. Ob
34. Harp
35. Snow Flake
36. San Miguel
37. Steinlager
38. Cisk Lager
39. Keo
40. Laziza
41. Ringnes
42. Fix

Country Of Origin

O. Nepal
P. New Zealand
Q. Lebanon
R. Portugal
S. Singapore
T. Malta
U. France
V. Switzerland
W. China
X. Yugoslavia
Y. Morocco
Z. Malaysia
AA. Indonesia
BB. Austria
CC. Denmark
DD. Israel
EE. Ireland
FF. Germany
GG. Italy
HH. Usa
II. Turkey
JJ. England
KK. Japan
LL. Egypt
MM. Canada
NN. India
OO. Belgium
PP. Greece

Answers

41 – J	33 – F	25 – X	17 – I	9 – HH	1 – C
42 – PP	34 – EE	26 – A	18 – FF	10 – MM	2 – S
	35 – W	27 – II	19 – BB	11 – R	3 – Z
	36 – H	28 – D	20 – V	12 – GG	4 – K
	37 – P	29 – DD	21 – Y	13 – U	5 – AA
	38 – T	30 – NN	22 – B	14 – OO	6 – L
	39 – N	31 – O	23 – W	15 – G	7 – JJ
	40 – Q	32 – KK	24 – LL	16 – CC	8 – E

Fix was the only beer ever brewed in Greece. Although the brewery went out of business in 1986, many a Greek can still remember with nostalgia walking into a bar, beating his fist on the counter and shouting, "Give me a Fix."
In those days, it had a different meaning!

Scenario Answer: Foster's is possibly Australia's most famous beer

The Bottom Line

Five years, fifty-one countries, 165,000 road miles. How much did it cost to make this ride?

I would like to say from the beginning that I was not sponsored at anytime during my ride. I paid for everything. If you're a rider and looking for a potential sponsor, you'll quickly discover, as I did, that all motorcycle manufacturers are notoriously tight-fisted when it comes to a promotion of this type. Perhaps it's because they receive so many requests from would-be world riders. Whatever the explanation, one thing is certain — unless your family name just happens to be Honda or Harley the figures that appear below are more or less what it will cost you to make this same trip.

Prior to the start of my ride, I had had visions of undergoing a starter motor overhaul on the bleak, windswept plateaus of Tibet. At other times, my nightmares would shift to the Sahara desert of North Africa, where, between sand dunes and under a blazing sun, I'd be doing a wheel-bearing changeout. To prevent these premonitions from becoming a reality, I decided not to chance fate, but to go with a sound preventative maintenance program, one in which the worn-out engine and frame parts would be replaced with new ones prior to an actual failure. Only once in all those years, and that occurred in India, did I foul-up in estimating the number of miles that I thought that I could get out of a clutch master cylinder. And what a place for a miscalculation!

- Motorcycle, Parts and Service $10,621
- Ocean Shipping and 7,150
  Air Fright Charges
  (7 times by sea, once by air)
- Eight Airline Tickets 5,258
- Cost of Living 48,000
  (Budget: $800 per month)

The Bottom Line **$71,029**

The Pit Stop

Our computers in Southern **California** contain far more information than can ever appear in any single edition of *The ENDLESS RIDE*. Therefore, if you have a special question, an unusual request, or would just like to pass along information useful to other riders, call, Fax or write. We welcome all corrections.

Address all mail to:
The Pit Stop
P. O. Box 10044
Newport Beach, CA 92658-0044
USA

Call or Fax:
Tel: (714) 760-3873
Fax: (714) 720-1230

Although we publish in more than one language, please address all correspondence in English.

Additional Copies

This book, *The ENDLESS RIDE*, is available from select Honda dealers and leading bookstores worldwide. If your dealer or bookstore is temporarily out, you may order directly from the publisher.

We accept Visa & Mastercard. Ask about Club Discounts. For information, on prices and shipping, see last page.

Phone, fax or write:
The ENDLESS RIDE Publications
Tel: (714) 760-3873
Fax: (714) 720-1230
P.O. Box 10044
Newport Beach,
CA 92658-0044, USA

Personal Ride Log

Date	Time	Place

Date	Time	Place

Date	Time	Place

Date	Time	Place

Date	Time	Place

Date	Time	Place

Date	Time	Place
____	____	_____
____	____	_____
____	____	_____
____	____	_____
____	____	_____
____	____	_____
____	____	_____
____	____	_____
____	____	_____
____	____	_____
____	____	_____
____	____	_____
____	____	_____
____	____	_____
____	____	_____